齊物
逍遙
2024 I

黃效文───

著

ENLIGHTENED
SOJOURN

Authored and Photographed by Wong How Man

Wong How Man

Time Magazine honored Wong How Man among their 25 Asian Heroes in 2002, calling Wong "China's most accomplished living explorer". CNN has featured his work over a dozen times, including a half-hour profile by the network's anchor. Discovery Channel has made several documentaries about his work. The Wall Street Journal has also featured him on its front page. Wong began exploring China in 1974. He is Founder/President of the China Exploration & Research Society, a non-profit organization founded in 1986 specializing in exploration, research, conservation and education in remote China and neighboring countries. Wong has led six major expeditions for the National Geographic. He successfully defined the sources of the Yangtze, Mekong, Yellow River, Salween, Irrawaddy and the Brahmaputra rivers.

He conducts projects in Mainland China, India, Nepal, Bhutan, Laos, Myanmar, the Philippines, and also Taiwan. In these countries or regions, he has set up centers, theme exhibits, or permanent operation bases. Wong has authored over thirty books and has received many accolades, among them an honorary doctorate from his alma mater, the University of Wisconsin at River Falls, and the Lifetime Achievement Award from Monk Hsing Yun of Taiwan. He has been invited as keynote speaker at many international functions.

In 2023, the University of Hong Kong established the Wong How Man Centre for Exploration in order to perpetuate the legacy of his work into the future.

黃
效
文

《時代雜誌》在二〇〇二年曾選黃效文為亞洲二十五位英雄之一，稱他為「中國最有成就的在世探險家」。*CNN* 報導過黃效文的各項工作超過十二次之多，其中還包括主播 *Richard Quest* 的三十分鐘專訪。探索頻道也為他做的工作製作了好幾個紀錄片。《華爾街日報》也曾用頭版報導過他。

黃效文自一九七四年開始在中國探險。他是中國探險學會的創辦人和會長，這是個非營利組織，致力於在中國偏遠地區及鄰近國家的探險、研究、保育和教育工作。他曾經在美國《國家地理雜誌》帶領過六個重要的探險。他成功地定位的源頭包括長江、湄公河、黃河、薩爾溫江、伊洛瓦底江及雅魯藏布江。

他的學會主導的文化和自然保育項目橫跨中國和鄰近的國家，包括印度、尼泊爾、不丹、寮國、緬甸、菲律賓還有台灣。

黃效文著作的書超過三十本並獲得過許多榮譽，他的母校威斯康辛大學頒發給他名譽博士學位，星雲大師也贈與他「華人世界終身成就獎」。他也是許多國際會議裡的專題演講人。

二〇二三年，香港大學成立了黃效文探險中心，以傳承他畢生的事業，並力圖讓他的精神與貢獻在未來繼續閃耀。

Foreword by George Yeo
Former Foreign Minister of Singapore

Enlightened Sojourn is a delicious collection of some of How Man's field reports over the last 50 years. He is a wonderful story teller. Through his accounts, we are invited to share his experiences of people and places. These are experiences we wish for ourselves but often can't have because they are off the beaten track and with individuals we only read about. His choice of photographs and liberal use of images from space and historic or modern maps, bring us close to the action.

Despite a half century in exploration, How Man does not grow old in spirit. His curiosity remains that of a young explorer. His enthusiasm is infectious. His delight in the richness of geography and culture reminds us that true beauty is to be found in diversity.

George Yeo & HM / 楊榮文（右）& HM

It was my good luck to know How Man after re-locating to work in Hong Kong. His reputation preceded him. I like to think we are kindred spirits although, despite being younger, I lack his physical energy or courage. An evening with him is always a pleasure and an education.

How Man inspires not by preaching or argument, but by perspective. Somehow the same reality seen through his lenses appears more interesting, joyous and hopeful. This is a perspective the world sorely needs today. Hong Kong University's decision to name a centre after How Man in order to inspire others to follow in his footsteps is indeed farsighted. It is all too easy to fixate on the negative in the world and see the problem in other human beings. A change in perspective enables us to see the beauty in nature and the beauty of man in nature. Enlightened Sojourn enriches us in this way.

序
新加坡前外交部長 楊榮文

《齊物逍遙》在我心中是一部令人心蕩神馳的珍藏品，這個系列匯集了黃效文先生過去五十年來探險工作的實地報告，而這本書凝結了他近期旅程的精華。

永遠不要懷疑他講故事的能力，因為他的文字總是那麼引人入勝。透過他的敘述，我們得以共用他在世界各地的奇妙經歷。這些經歷是我夢寐以求但往往難以實現的，因為他們太偏離常軌，那些與之產生聯繫的人物，我彷彿只能在書中才能和其相遇。同時，書中那些精心挑選的照片，結合大量使用的衛星影像以及古今地圖，讓我們彷彿置身於那些生動的場景中，能近距離感受那份真實的震撼。

儘管半個世紀的探險生涯已匆匆過去，黃效文先生依然保持著旺盛的好奇心和極具感染力的熱情。他對地理和文化的追求提醒著我們，真正的美麗存在於多樣性之中。他是真正具有探險精神的人。

能夠認識黃效文先生是我的幸運。早在我搬到香港工作之前，就久聞他的盛名。我們有著志同道合的靈魂，儘管我比他年輕，卻缺乏他的精力與勇氣。每個能與他坐下來交談的夜晚都是那麼愉快又充滿教育意義。

黃效文先生對我的啟發並非來自說教的言詞或是銳利的辯論，而是來自他看待這個世界的視角。透過他的鏡頭，我能看到原本千篇一律的現實世界變得更加有趣、令人愉悅並且充滿希望。這正是當今世界迫切需要的視野。

香港大學決定以黃效文先生的名字命名一個探險交流中心，確實是高瞻遠矚的決策。不斷變化的社會環境迫使現在的人太容易執著於負面，並將問題歸咎他人。黃效文先生的精神能激勵我們追隨他的腳步，轉變視角，從而看到自然本身的美麗和身處自然中的人類所散發的人性美。《齊物逍遙》正是以這種方式啟迪了我們的心靈。

Preface

This special series of books, all with the same title of Enlightened Sojourn, is now into its sixth and seventh volume. They recount my travels and reflections. In the past, it used to come out as one book per year. With my waning years in energy and thus travel frequency, I expected that it would ultimately take two years of sojourn to compile one book, enlightened or not.

But not quite. Suddenly I found that after the pandemic, and four rounds of quarantine during that period in order to continue my fieldwork, I am squeezing more and more time to get into the field. It is as if I am trying to make up for time lost, as well as packing in as much field time as possible while counting down toward my own expiration date and lapsing eventually into obscurity.

Whatever reasons they may be, the sojourn for last year ended up not necessarily the most productive, yet resulting in a very diverse coverage in both latitude and longitude. As one volume, it would be way too long for a small-format book. Thus it is decided to split it into two books, Book 1 and Book 2, which I present herewith for my friends, supporters, and select readers.

Perhaps it is worth mentioning that I have often felt I am writing for myself, as a reminiscence and record of my own life and experience. If by chance it is read and appreciated by others, all the better. But I have never intended it as a popular publication for the mass market.

The illustrations, through images that I took, are often prompters to remind me of what I may want to write about. In some ways, I did not take pictures with my eyes, but my mind. That is a tradition and practice I have devised as my own style, and followed as early as during my stint at the National Geographic some forty years ago. It has served me well. As whatever dramatic experience I have encountered, I seem to have the picture to illustrate it, as fact rather than fiction.

I hope my readers would enjoy the stories as much as I would reminiscence these experiences, trivial as some may be.

前言

《齊物逍遙》這一系列特別書籍，現已進入第六本和第七本。這些書記載了我多年來的經歷與反思。過去，我每年都會出版一本書。然而隨著年事漸高，精力和旅行頻率逐漸減少，我原以為現階段完成一本書至少需要兩年的時間。

但事實是，疫情期間，我經歷了四次隔離，以期繼續做野外工作。這讓我愈發感慨時間的寶貴。於是疫情後，我開始更加努力地擠出時間進行野外工作，彌補失去的時光。生命的終點任何人都無法預測和左右，我只想在還能工作的日子裡，盡可能多地進行實地探索。

去年一整年的旅程雖然並非最具成效，但在緯度和經度上卻涵蓋了非常廣泛而多樣的範圍。若將其合併成一本書，會顯得過於冗長。因此，我決定將其分為兩本，即上下兩集，呈獻給我的朋友、支持者和精選的讀者們。

我常覺得我是在為自己而寫作，過程像在給自己留下一把回憶的鑰匙。如果這些文字偶然被他人閱讀並欣賞，那自然是極好的，但我從未打算將大眾市場的流行度作為衡量我作品的標準和追求。

每次我按下快門時，並非是用眼睛在拍照，而是在用我的頭腦和心靈。這就是為什麼我時常是先翻到照片，再開始寫文字。書中的那些圖像，常常會提醒我想要表達什麼。這是我在四十年前於美國《國家地理雜誌》工作時期便養成的習慣，一直以來對我幫助良多。無論我經歷了多麼戲劇性的事情，似乎總有影像來佐證這些經歷的絕對真實。

儘管本書中可能存在大量瑣碎的細節，但我仍希望讀者能夠像我回憶這些經歷時一樣，享受並從中解讀出積極的意義。

目次

後疫情與後政變下，說說緬甸

POST-PANDEMIC & POST-COUP MYANMAR RANTING

Mandalay, Myanmar – September 20, 2022

Mandalay, Myanmar – September 20, 2022

POST-PANDEMIC & POST-COUP MYANMAR RANTING

"If you cannot change the situation, change your attitude." That's something I have shared with students many times before. So here I am, back in Mandalay, where CERS has our boat and houses. Sanctions? That's a game the big guys play on the little kids. Remember Theodore Roosevelt : "Speak softly and carry a big stick," his oft-repeated foreign policy message. And that remark is now over a hundred years old, and repeatedly acted upon, though not always successful anymore.

Kids are still kids here, playing after school into the evening, even into the darkness of night when supply of electricity is at times sporadic with blackouts. Our village, Thapatetann, is a weaving and pottery village at a confluence with the Irrawaddy. The weaving machines are running its "clicking clicking" sound all day, the potter's wheels are still turning. Autumn dragonflies flapping their wings and little squirrels bounce among late season mango fruits on the tree. But intellectuals and educated people, or those pretending to be so, are angry and troubled. Angry with both nature and humankind, angry that Covid should descend upon us and troubled by an untimely military coup.

In attitude, I too have changed, hiding my frustration as I went through two swab tests, one in Bangkok Airport in order to check in for my flight and a second one upon landing in Mandalay. As to post-coup measures, there is curfew by 8:00 PM and I must cross the Irrawaddy Bridge and be in my hotel before dark. Though we have our boat and house-base by the river, it is advised not to stay there during turbulent times.

Neither are we welcome by some villagers, who may be paranoid of outsiders during Covid and politically testing times, be it nature- or human-imposed. And during troubled times, there are always those who enjoy reporting on others to gain the little merit they could muster. In times of peace and stability, those are usually the most insignificant vermin and scum of a society.

Village sunset scene / 村莊裡的日落景象

Business as usual? Not quite, as tourism, which many developing countries and emerging markets depended heavily on, has dried up over the last two and a half years. The only consolation is that this time it is global, sparing no one, be it a country in the first or third world, Orient or Occident, North or South hemisphere.

Enough intellectual and smart blurb from your writer here.

After one night in a hotel with my colleagues across the Irrawaddy in Sagaing, I decided to risk the curse of the vermin, and stayed for the night in my tiny upstairs room in our house. Nothing happened, and I had a sound sleep. Come morning, I spent time decorating our meeting room with new paintings we recently acquired before my colleagues rejoined me to embark on a cruise in a small wooden boat upriver for a little birdwatching. That had been my routine over the years.

While having my hot chocolate sitting at our balcony, I observed for over an hour our boatman trying to start our long-tailed engine for the boat. It has not been used for over two years and the inside must be rusted. Su, our field biologist, arrives in time to offer an engine she has bought recently, second hand. She paid one Lakh (US$32) in order to help a family in need. A new engine would have cost three times as much. The old engine kicks up upon the first pull, better than our rather new but unused one. An ironic lesson for those of us who keep plenty of money, or branded luxuries, unused.

Not many birds are sighted as winter has not set in yet and migrating flocks have not yet arrived.

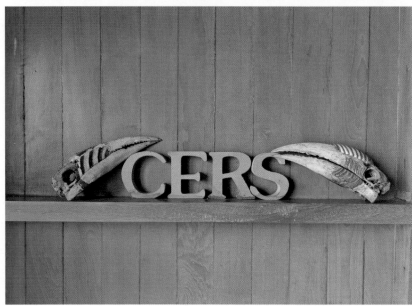

Paintings at meeting room / 會議室裡的畫作
CERS with hornbill beaks / 犀鳥嘴

Kingfisher / 翠鳥

I spot two common kingfishers, as their blue turquoise coat is easy to distinguish. One Little Cormorant, three kites and three Vinous-breasted Starlings make up my list for the morning. As usual, egrets are so common I never count them as sightings.

As fuel become of shortage and more pricey, more boats are going retro, being rowed rather than running with the long-tail motor. We stop beside a boat as two men are pulling up the net. No catch this round, but earlier in the morning, they caught a palm-length Short-headed Catfish and a half-kilo carp, locally called nga-net-pya. We bought both for our lunch at 7000 Kyat; barely US$2 at current black market exchange rate but over US$5 at bank rate. I ask the fisherman Aung Myo Oo (46) how the yield has been in recent years. "Much fewer than two years ago," he answers. His son Yae Tshan is 18 and helping his father on the boat, since not much work is available anywhere these days.

Inflation has hit hard, and prices are escalating by the day. Starting a year ago in September, CERS regularly dispatches rice and cooking oil within the village we set up as base. For five months, we have given out each month 13 bags of rice, each bag weighing 24 byi or 31 kilos, at a cost of 35,000 kyat (US$25) per bag. Our budget for giving is only US$500 per month. Today, the same bag of rice is more than double, costing 75,000 kyat. Our carpenter Tin Aung reflects that teak has gone up from 12 Lakh (US$900) per ton to now 18 Lakh, a 50% hike. Since our contract with him was made before Covid, his labor charges remain at 10,000 Kyat per day than the current rate of 15,000. Enough numbers crunching from your pseudo-economist.

I receive a daily report from an international security outfit regarding Myanmar. In report #675 yesterday evening, formerly peaceful and tranquil Ma Sein village by the Chindwin River where we had picked up a cat and have a pagoda built nearby at the Tropic of Cancer is making the long list of places to avoid. It was in 2014 that the CERS newsletter ran a cover story on Ma Sein. On 18 September 2022, around 05:00 Hrs, in Kalewa Township (Sagaing Region), an unknown group attacked and set fire to a police outpost in Ma Sein Village; 7 police officers and a police chief's son were reportedly killed, some arms and ammunition were seized. An explorer is not a war or frontline correspondent. My team have to manage risk and avoid the countryside for a while to come. Our HM Explorer boat, with seven cabins, would likewise be moored to our premises for a while to come.

Like the fish that is becoming less abundant, the trash that used to float down the river all day long is also becoming less, as far as I could see. That,

Newsletter cover / 通訊封面

perhaps because money is tight and less refuse is generated. But I must give credit also to our own CERS team members who have used the pandemic to work closely with their immediate community by providing bamboo-woven trash bins to villages along the river. They have also started a campaign to educate children and parents to stop them throwing their trash into the river. Such small projects may also be yielding some results.

For lunch, we have the cat fish steamed. It is delicious and fresh. While eating, I ponder, as everything is becoming less, what about the monks who go from household to household each morning to collect alms in the form of food. Are they too receiving less? But perhaps such a question, in a country where monks are highly respected, would be better left unanswered.

And respect and etiquette I must learn and maintain. Momentarily, Sandra our Country Manager passes me the paper napkin box, reminding me that I should stop pulling up my longyi, the traditional Myanmar men's skirt, to wipe my mouth at the table. But old habits are hard to change, not unlike the sunrise and sunset each day I can view from our Mandalay House.

Minga-labar!

HM in longyi with Sandra & Su / 身穿長裙的 HM 與桑德拉 & 蘇

後疫情與後政變下，說說緬甸

「如果你無法改變現狀，那就改變你的態度。」這是我多年來經常與學生分享的一番話。於是，我又回來了，回到緬甸的曼德勒，因為這裡有「中國探險學會」所設置的工作船與工作基地。制裁？那是一群大人對付小孩的遊戲。記得美國前任總統羅斯福 *(Theodore Roosevelt)* 說過的那句「大棒子」名言嗎？——「說話要輕聲細語，但手上拿根大棒子。」老總統堅信不移的外交政策，已跨越百年歷史，即使未必總是成功如願，卻經得起大時代的驗證與應用。

孩子終究是孩子，放學後就只想貪玩到晚，即使黑夜中常因電力供應不足而停電，也不肯錯過玩樂。我們的所在地，塔帕特坦 *(Thapatetann)*，是個以織布與製陶為主的村莊，位於伊洛瓦底江的匯合處。織布機的喀嚓喀嚓聲，日以繼夜，不停放送；製陶的輪子也不分日夜地轉動。秋天到訪的蜻蜓拍翅飛翔，小松鼠繞著採收近尾聲的芒果與樹幹間，來去無蹤地蹦跳。但街上的飽學之士或自以為是的知識分子，則書空咄咄，憤怒又不安。無論自然界或人類都令他們憤恨不平，惱怒該來的新冠肺炎為何遲遲未現身，也對一場不合時宜的軍事政變惴惴不安。

以態度來說，我也開始改變了，尤其在我體驗過兩次新冠肺炎的檢測後——一次在曼谷機場辦理登機前，另一次是抵達曼德勒機場準備入境時。我把滿懷的挫折感埋在心

底，藏起來。政變以後，晚上八點開始宵禁，而我必須穿越伊洛瓦底江大橋，風塵僕僕趕在天黑前抵達下榻的飯店。雖然大江河畔有我們的工作船與基地工作室，但我們都知道在時局動盪期間，最好不要待在那裡。

我們的到訪不受當地村民待見，那其實也無可厚非，因為新冠肺炎的疫情與政局動亂的考驗，無論是不可控的疫情或人為的擾亂，都難免令村民對外來者有所保留。風雨飄搖時，總有人喜歡見縫插針，一心想撈到些好處。但在風平浪靜時，這些機會主義者通常是社會中最無足輕重的社會渣滓與害蟲。

生意照舊？不盡然，因為許多發展中國家與新興市場極度賴以為生的旅遊業，在過去兩年半內已彈盡糧絕。唯一稍稍值得安慰的是，這波疫情的延燒擴及全球，沒有任何國家得以倖免，無論你位處世界頂端或第三世界，不管你在東方或西方、北半球或南半球，沒有任何一方躲過疫情這一劫。

不過，這倒是讓許多知識分子與聰明人士有機可乘，大作文章了。

我和同行夥伴在伊洛瓦底江對岸的實皆 *(Sagaing)* 城過了一夜後，我決定冒著被社會害蟲詛咒的風險，跑回我們學會的基地，在工作室的頂樓小房住一晚。我一夜好眠，安然無事。隔天清晨，我

Village lady sewing / 縫紉中的村婦
Kids playing / 玩耍的孩子們

Fishing / 釣魚

花了些時間把最近取得的新畫作，掛在我們的會議室牆上；當同事過來這裡與我會合後，我們便搭乘小木船出發，往河上賞鳥。這是我多年來養成的慣例。

回來後，我坐在陽台上品嚐一杯熱巧克力，一邊觀察我們的船夫，我看他一個多小時以來不斷試著啟動我們的長尾船引擎。這部引擎已擱置沒用超過兩年，內部結構肯定鏽蝕了。我們的田野生物學家蘇 (Su)，及時趕到現場，把她最近剛購入的二手引擎一起帶來。這是她為了幫助一個亟需救助的家庭而花了十萬拉克（折合約三十二美元）買來的引擎；如果要買一台全新引擎，至少比這價格貴三倍。雖是二手貨，但船夫一發動便成了，遠比之前那部嶄新卻沒用多少次的引擎還要好得多。眼前一幕，對我們當中保存大量金錢或名牌奢侈品卻從不使用的許多人來說，真是個當頭棒喝。

冬天未到，遷徙的候鳥還沒報到，所以能看的鳥也不多。我發現了兩隻尋常的翠鳥，牠們一身藍色綠松石的外衣，辨識度很高。另外還有一隻小鸕鶿，外加三隻鳶與三隻紅嘴椋鳥，這就是我當天上午的賞鳥收穫。一如往常，我沒有把隨處可見的白鷺視為我的觀察目標。

隨著燃料短缺與居高不下的價格，越來越多船隻開始走向復古

風，不再使用長尾馬達而紛紛改用「人工」划槳。我們在一艘船邊停下，船上兩人正在收網。看來這一輪是一無所獲了，但更早之前，他們已捕獲一尾巴掌長的短頭鯰魚，和一條半公斤重的鯉魚，當地人稱之為 *nga-net-pya*。我們花了七千緬元 (折合約兩美元) 買下他們的兩條魚，為我們的午餐做準備。按照緬甸當前的黑市匯率是將近兩美元，但若到銀行去兌換，則要超過五美元。我開口詢問四十六歲的其中一位漁夫翁摩武 *(Aung Myo Oo)*，最近幾年的漁獲產量如何？「比兩年前少得多。」他回答。身邊十八歲的兒子葉梓山，因為這段日子找不到什麼工可做，只好在船上協助父親捕魚。

源於通貨膨脹的衝擊，物價也跟著日益飆漲。從一年前的九月開始，「中國探險學會」在我們設置基地的村子裡，定期發放大米與食用油給村民。近五個月來，每月平均發放十三袋大米，每袋重量三十一公斤，一包米的價格是三萬五千緬元 (折合約二十五美元)。我們計畫每月捐贈的預算只有五百美元。今天，一袋大米的價格已翻漲超過一倍，來到七萬五千緬元。我們的木匠丁昂 *(Tin*

Starlings & dragonfly / 椋鳥與蜻蜓

Kite / 鳶

Yae Tshan with fish / 葉梓山與剛抓到的魚

HM Explorer at night / 夜晚的 HM Explorer 考察船

Cat fish served / 盛盤的鯰魚
My 1962 Land Rover / 1962 路虎

Aung) 向我們反映，柚木價格從原來的一噸十二拉克（折合約九百美元），一漲就漲到十八拉克，漲幅高達百分之五十。我們是在疫情前和他簽訂合約，所以，他的工資依舊維持每日一萬緬元，而非現在每日一萬五千緬元的工資行情。外面這群在市場上搞數據運算的假冒經濟大師啊，你們玩得過頭了吧！

我每天都會收到來自國際安全組織寄來有關緬甸的報告。昨晚一份 #675 期的報告內容提及，伊洛瓦底江最大支流欽敦江 (Chindwin) 旁，屬於實皆城的卡勒瓦 (Kalewa) 鎮裡的馬賢村 (Ma Sein)，於二〇二二年九月十八日五點左右，有間警察局遭身分不明的團體襲擊與放火；據報導，七名警員與一名警長的兒子被殺，部分武器與彈藥也被搶走。其實，我們對馬賢村並不陌生。「中國探險學會」的通訊曾在二〇一四年刊載一篇關於馬賢村的封面故事。這裡曾是個安閒平靜的村莊，我們還曾在此撿過一隻貓，也在鄰近的北回歸線附近蓋了座佛塔，但現在這個地方已被列為「應避免前往」的紅色警戒區。像我這樣一位探險工作者，既不是戰地記者，也不是跑前線的新聞工作者。但我們的團隊仍須謹慎面對風險管理的議題，並在未來的一段時間內，盡可能避免待在鄉下。我們的考察船 HM Explorer 內置七個船艙，在這段情勢未明時，只能停泊於駐地。

除了河裡的漁獲量減少，就我看來，過去河上隨處可見的漂浮垃

坂，也比過去少多了。也許因為錢少購物少而產生的垃圾量也跟著大幅減少。不過，我還是要把部分功勞歸功於我們「中國探險學會」的團隊成員——他們善用疫情當機會教育，與當地社區居民密切合作，向河流沿岸村莊提供竹編垃圾桶。他們還開辦兒童與家長的教育活動，強化公共衛生概念，灌輸村民切勿把垃圾扔進河裡。這些小小的計畫與行動，想必也帶來一些成效。

直接和漁夫採購的那隻鯰魚，清蒸料理後成了我們的午餐。肉鮮味美。我邊吃邊想，當所有資源都捉襟見肘時，那些每早挨家挨戶托缽乞食的僧人，該怎麼辦？他們碗裡的東西，是不是也更少了？不過，在這個對僧侶高度敬重的國度，這樣的問題或許就不便去問了。

看來，尊重與禮節，恐怕才是我必須學習與保有的吧。我在用餐時，身穿緬甸男性的傳統長裙，不一會兒，我們的「緬甸經理」桑德拉 (Sandra) 把餐巾盒遞給我，提示我不要在餐桌上再拉起我的長裙擦嘴了。不過，我看我真是「積習難改」了，仿若我每天在曼德勒之家望出去的日出日落一樣，那麼自然來去，天經地義。

Minga-labar!

Burnt 1962 LR / 被燒掉的路虎

在北婆羅洲跳島（上）

ISLAND HOPPING IN NORTH BORNEO (Part 1)

Kudat, Sabah – October 11, 2022

ISLAND HOPPING IN NORTH BORNEO (Part 1)
At sea, on land, and half way in between

Within one afternoon, I ran into two unusual beings. One at sea, the other, half way between land and sea. The first was a red and white banded seahorse I named "Red Zebra". Our encounter lasted just a few minutes, as he had to be put back into the sea urgently, as it, or "he", was not only a member of a species highly threatened with extinction but was also pregnant and ready to give birth. He came into my hands from the seabed, from among a few hundred big and small fish and sea-creatures caught when our fishing boat pulled up its huge net.

Every few seconds, Red Zebra would make a tiny "clicking" sound while his body went into a jerk, straightening both his head and curled tail at the same time. His belly bulged out showing its pregnancy. With seahorses, a male gets pregnant when a female, after mating, deposits her eggs into a brood pouch in the front belly of the male. These fertilized eggs would be brooded by the male until ready for delivery. They would then be discharged from the pouch in squirts, with each squirt dispatching hundreds of baby seahorses into the sea.

Actually, over ninety percent of our catch in the net would be shuffled back into the ocean through a hole in the back deck, with us saving only a tiny portion, those that are more palatable, for the

HM with Seahorse / HM 與海馬

dinner table. On this round of raising the net after towing it for over an hour at sea, we kept quite a few shells of scallop, half a dozen prawns, squids, a couple of small ray fish, a flounder, a large blue crab and some palm-sized fish.

I am at the stern of fishing boat KT3295F (most fishing boats do not have names, just registration numbers), which I have chartered for four days. "Big Blue", as I named the boat, is captained and manned by two young brothers, Anil (30) and Pedy (29). Two days ago, our catch was much larger, perhaps two hundred kilos or more when dumped on the deck, filling up a very large space. At first sight, it was as if we had pulled up a lot of ping pong balls inside the net. On closer inspection, these proved to be hundreds of small puffer fish, puffing up and inflating their bellies once disturbed.

Momentarily, an analogy came into mind. China has been closing its net on corruption. At first, media in the West kept reporting it as only for eradication of top political enemies. Now, the anti-corruption policy has been going on for years, bringing to justice even those who has been retired for years as the net closes tighter and tighter,

Catch with ping pong puffer fish /
抓到乒乓球似的河豚
Kudat fish market / 古達漁市

defying predications and accusations by many so-called "China watchers". But since people these days have short memories, we never hold these political fortunetellers accountable for their wrong speculations, and they continue to interpret actions of China, as well as elsewhere.

Like the ping-pongs in our net, those inflating themselves to show off are caught early on. The smaller fish somehow would get out from the wide holes of our net. However, there are always a flock of gulls and terns circling behind our fishing boat when the net is pulled, scavenging on such half-stunned remains. Simple reality can at times reflect political scenario.

Another analogy is perhaps more cute and appealing. Seahorses have been featured in at least two of Disney's most popular movies, Finding Nemo and Little Mermaid, with characters like Sheldon and Herald respectively. And the mermaid is believed to be a mythical sea creature derived from the Dugong, an occasional visitor in waters around here. This very tame marine mammal is also known as the Sea Cow; not so romantic as a mermaid.

At every fishing village I visited, I asked about the Dugong hoping to see this large marine mammal, with adults growing to three meters and weighing half a ton. Local fishermen said they are most active during early

Anil at bow / 在船頭上的的阿尼爾
Pedy at bridge / 在駕駛艙裡的裴狄

spring, and are often seen coming to the surface with newborn babies. As I arrived out of season, I opted to keep my imagination alive by photographing a simulated Dugong reflected off coral reefs when I did a bit of snorkeling.

The other encounter on this same day was with someone named Fidel, a teacher from Kuala Lumpur but living for thirteen years in a small stilt house edging on the ocean of Malawili Island. The house is rented from Toton for a meager 300 MYR (equivalent of USD 64) a month. We spent the night sleeping at Toton's house, right behind Fidel's, on the living room floor, and for free.

Fidel speaks perfect English, which is what he is teaching at the only school in Malawili. The school covers six grades of elementary, but has only 25 students. For high school, students will attend

Teacher's home / 老師的家

Grandchild of Nasirin / 納斯霖的孫子

boarding school on the larger island of Karakit. There are a total of nine teachers at the Malawili School, a ratio of 2.5 students to each teacher, beating the best private schools I know of, like Lawrenceville and Deerfield in the US, or Winchester and Cheltenham Ladies in the UK.

Fidel was a bit shy when he found out I was a journalist, so I asked few questions and just let him talk. "I love this place, but after thirteen years, I would like to go home to Kuala Lumpur," he said. "But the principal is so very nice to me so I decided to stay on until they can find an appropriate replacement."

Since Malawili is surrounded on all sides by coral reef, the houses seem to stay firm even though supported by just a few stilts, as the reef can stop the sea waves from coming close. This should be a paradise for diving and snorkeling lovers, though few people have heard about it. I showed a picture of me holding Red Zebra and asked Fidel if he had ever seen one. "No, never have I seen such a beautiful seahorse," came his answer. I suddenly felt even more lucky to have held one in my hand, though only for a brief moment.

Malawili Island's singular village has only 42 families. Freshwater supply has always been precious and in short supply, until recently. May Bank of

Malaysia has donated dozens of huge water tanks to collect rainwater for the community. The people here subsist on fishing. There are a few older gentlemen wearing little white caps. These are members with the title of Haji, men who have made their pilgrimage to Mecca.

Toton's father Nasirin has a big family. They have the largest and longest house in the village. The front section, facing the village, is the only market shop on the island, selling noodles, canned food, beverages and other sundry products. Each family has one or two wooden speedboats, used for fishing or as transport. Everyone buys their supply of gasoline from Nasirin. The shop is connected to the main house with dining area and many bedrooms, as their extended family all live here.

Currently, Toton is finishing construction of a new house, right next to the small house he rented out to Fidel. As with all houses at Malawili, the kitchen and bathroom face the sea with makeshift drainage; just a hole into the vast ocean. Seaview is not considered a prime choice, as the ocean is their immediate neighbor on all sides, including below the houses.

At high tide in the evening, I can see many fish, large and small, swimming right below the house and in between the stilts, probably feasting from what came down from our houses.

Toton with fish caught / 托頓與抓到的魚
Kudat fishing boat / 古達漁船

在北婆羅洲跳島（上）

水上與陸地，還有水陸之間

才一個下午，我便遇見兩個非比尋常的生命個體。一個在水裡，一個在水陸之間。首先是一隻紅白相間的帶狀海馬，我給牠取名「紅斑馬」。我們之間的相遇只持續數分鐘，因為牠的狀況十分危急，需要趕緊被放回海裡；牠或「他」，不僅是高度瀕危物種，而且還有孕在身，隨時準備生產。這隻紅斑馬從海底到我手中之前，其實和數百條大小魚等海洋生物一起擠身於我們拉起來的巨大漁網中。

每隔幾秒，紅斑馬便發出微弱的「喀嚓」聲，伴隨身體一陣抽搐，同時把頭部與捲曲的尾巴拉伸打直。他的肚子鼓脹，顯然是懷孕了。當雌雄海馬交配後，雌海馬把受精卵置入雄海馬腹部前方類似育兒袋的孵卵囊中，後續的孵育胚胎與懷孕分娩等大工程，都是海馬爸爸的事了。產期一到，海馬爸爸會從育兒袋中噴出寶寶，數百隻海馬寶寶就這樣被「噴」入海中。

其實，我們這一網漁獲，有超過百分之九十的大小海洋生物都會從甲板上的一個洞口，被放回海裡，我們只把其中可煮食的部分，保留起來當晚餐。這一輪在海上拖網一個多小時後，我們保留當食物的漁獲包括一些扇貝、六、七隻大蝦、魷魚、幾尾小魟魚、一尾比目魚、一隻大藍蟹和幾隻手掌大小的魚。

我坐在 *KT3295F* 漁船船尾處（這裡大部分漁船沒有船名，只有註冊號碼），靜觀眼前一切。這是我租下的船，未來四天，我都可以自由使用這艘被我取名「大藍」的漁船。船長與船員是一對年輕兄弟，分別是三十歲的阿尼爾與二十九歲的裴狄。我們兩天前的收穫比今天多，收網後撒在甲板上的漁獲量，至少超過兩百多公斤，佔滿好大一片空間。第一眼乍看下，網子裡似乎裝滿了不計其數的乒乓球；但仔細一看，這些一顆顆圓鼓鼓的生物，其實是數百隻小河豚，因為被我們擾攘而本能地把肚子鼓脹了氣。

我的腦海裡瞬間閃過一個比喻。一直以來，中國對貪腐問題保持收網的嚴辦決心。最初，西方媒體不斷指稱那是剷除高層政治對敵的手段。現在，反貪腐政策已持續好幾年，嚴懲的捕網，越收越緊，甚至不放過那些已退休多年的貪官污吏，將他們繩之以法，公然打臉那些所謂「中國觀察家」的預測與評論。只不過，現代人記憶力太差了，我們從未讓這些大放厥詞的政治算命師為自己的不當猜疑與言論負起責任，於是，他們繼續肆無忌憚地揣測中國的行動，甚至把攻擊觸角伸入其他領域。

一如我們網中的「乒乓球」，那些為了炫耀而自我膨脹者，總是最先被捕捉。體型較小的魚總是有辦法從我們的漁網鑽出去而成漏網之魚。不過，當我們開始奮力收網時，總有一群海鷗和燕鷗在漁

Dugong in real / 儒艮　　　　　　　　　　　　Tern scavenger / 燕鷗

船後方盤旋低飛，對著掙扎的魚蝦，虎視眈眈，亟欲叼食。簡單不過的現況，有時也能如實反映政治情事。

另一個類比，或許比較可愛和引人注目。海馬曾經出現在最受歡迎的兩部迪士尼電影中——各別在《海底總動員》和《小美人魚》裡飾演海馬東東 (Sheldon) 與小海赫 (Herald) 的角色。一直以來，大家把美人魚視為神話世界中的海洋生物，但其實牠的中文俗名為「儒艮」，很難得才會現身這片水域，是性格溫順、也被稱為「海牛」的海生哺乳類生物。經過科學分析的理性敘述後，頓時少了幾分想像中屬於美人魚的浪漫色彩。

我每到一個漁村，都會特別探聽一些「儒艮」的相關議題，一心期待能親眼看到這類大隻的海生哺乳類物種；據我所知，一般成年的儒艮，身長可達三公尺，重量有半噸。根據當地漁夫的說法，早春時分是儒艮最活躍的季節，經常可看到母儒艮帶著新生幼兒浮出水面。不過，我抵達當地時，早已過了春季，大概是無緣看到牠們了，看來，只能在浮潛時拍一張反射在珊瑚礁上的「儒艮模擬圖」來安慰自己，然後，把儒艮的

Fidel the teacher / 費德老師

School at Malawili / 馬拉維利島的學校

Nasirin at home / 納斯霖

想像存放心底，繼續前進。

同一天的另一個際遇，是認識了費德，一名來自馬來西亞首都吉隆坡的老師，在海角邊的馬拉維利 (Malawili) 島上一間小小高腳屋裡，一住就是十三年。這房子是費德跟當地村民托頓承租的，每月只需支付馬幣三百元(折合約六十四美元)租金。我們在托頓家住一晚，托頓的房子就在費德家正後方；我們是住免費的，大夥兒就睡在客廳地板上。

費德說得一口流利英文，所以他能在馬拉維利島上唯一的學校任教。這所學校涵蓋小學六個年級，全校只有二十五名學生。孩子們小學畢業後，若要升上中學，就得轉到另一個更大島加拉吉 (Karakit) 的寄宿學校就讀。馬拉維利島這所唯一的小學，共有九名教師，大約是一名老師對二點五名學生的比例，學生所享有的「教育資源與權益」，已比我曾到校演講過的最好的私校還要好得多——包括美國的羅倫斯威爾 (Lawrenceville) 中學、迪爾菲爾德 (Deerfield) 學院或英國的溫徹斯特公學 (Winchester)、切爾滕納姆女子中學 (Cheltenham Ladies)。

當費德發現我曾當過記者後，開始有些羞怯，所以我盡量少發問，讓他自由表達。「我熱愛這個地方，但過了十三年後，我開始想要回老家吉隆坡了。」費德繼續說道：「但校長對我非常好，所以我決定留下來，一直到他們找到合適的人替代我的工作。」

雖然當地高腳屋看似地基單薄，但馬拉維利島的四面八方都是珊瑚礁環繞，所以房子還算穩固，因為珊瑚礁可以阻擋海浪太靠近。雖然這島嶼沒沒無聞，但確實是潛水與浮潛愛好者的天堂。我拿出一張「手捧紅斑馬」的照片給費德看，問他是否見過。「沒有啊，我從來沒見過那麼美的海馬。」他的回應讓我覺得自己實在太幸運，此生竟曾緊握如此迷人的懷孕海馬，哪怕只是短暫的剎那，也

足以讓我欣慰。

馬拉維利島的唯一村莊，只有四十二戶家庭。淡水供應向來比較短缺，所以特別珍貴；直到最近，供水才越來越穩定。馬來西亞最大的商業銀行「馬來亞銀行」(Maybank) 捐贈了數十個超級大水箱，讓社區島民可以收集雨水，儲水備用。這裡的居民以捕魚為生；走在島嶼上，偶爾瞥見幾位年紀較長、頭戴小白帽的先生，他們是曾到過麥加朝聖的穆斯林，因為完成朝覲而「晉升」為哈吉 (Haji) 身分。

托頓的父親納斯霖有個大家庭要照顧。村子裡最大、最長的房子，就是他們家的房子。面向村莊最前方的一排，是島上唯一的市場與店鋪，這裡可以買得到麵食、罐頭、飲品與其他雜貨。每一個家庭都有一兩艘木製快艇，是村民用來捕魚或代步的交通工具。納斯霖是村裡的獨家汽油供應商，所有居民都只能向他買汽油。汽油店和納斯霖的房子緊密相連，包括用餐區和很多房間，他們一大家族的成員，都住在這裡。

目前，托頓的新房子建設已進入尾聲，新房就在他租給費德的小屋隔壁。托頓的新房子和島上其他房屋格局大同小異，廚房與浴室都面向大海，還附上臨時的排水系統；其實，所謂排水，就是在地板上挖了個洞口，讓一切通往大海。至於有沒有海景，其實不是島嶼的重點，因為你無論怎麼環顧四周，都是一望無際的海，就算你躲到高腳屋下方，再怎麼轉身，觸目所及也都是一片海景。

傍晚漲潮，各種大小魚群在屋下和高腳樓之間游來游去，往下俯瞰時，看得一清二楚，我猜，或許魚兒正圍繞著從房子裡「流洩出去」的東西，爭相搶食而大快朵頤呢！

HM on Big Blue / HM 在「大藍」上

在北婆羅洲跳島（下）

ISLAND HOPPING IN NORTH BORNEO (Part 2)

Kuda, Sabah – October 11, 2022

ISLAND HOPPING IN NORTH BORNEO (Part 2)
At sea, on land, and half way in between

I would not have met Red Zebra the seahorse, Fidel the teacher or his landlord Toton, had it not been for someone I met ten days before. He was the most crucial person I chanced upon on this entire trip to northern Borneo. Without him, there would have been no fishing boat to charter, no islands to visit, no fishing villages to explore.

It was early morning on October 1 at 6am. In Beijing, this is the time of the ceremonial flag raising in front of Tien An Men Square, especially important on this day, the 73rd National Day of the PRC. (Year-round, the timing of this ceremony fluctuates based on time of sunrise.) I looked out my window facing the ocean and saw three fishing boats passing by, returning from a night of fishing at sea. The boats' waterlines were riding low and the bows were not pointed high, signifying that they had a good haul of harvest. I decided to rush out to the jetty to see their catch, as well as getting to know the captains or owners of these boats.

The day before, upon my arrival at Kudat, we had hung around the marina jetty hoping to find a boat for charter in order to explore nearby islands; the main goal of my trip. No luck, as hardly anyone at the jetty could speak English; they were all Malay. Nearby were islands connected to

Fishing boat returns to port / 準備回港的漁船　　　　　　Mr Ho / 何萬發先生

those we have visited at the southern tip of Palawan around Balabac Island of the southern Philippines. Both the islands here in Malaysia at the north of Borneo, as well as those in Palawan, fringed on the sensitive Spratlys, tiny islands and atolls of the South China Sea. I wanted to get to know the people and surroundings of this area.

As baskets full of fresh caught fish, prawn and crab were hauled to land and put on awaiting pick-up trucks, I again struck up a conversation with an older Malay man, obviously owner of one of the fishing boats. He drew a blank, as again he could not understand what I was trying to get at. I turned around and suddenly saw a Chinese-looking man with his face mask on. I bravely uttered some Mandarin Chinese to greet him, hoping that he could help me translate.

It turned out that this man not only could speak Mandarin but was totally fluent in Cantonese as well. Ho Bang Huat, or Man-Fat in Cantonese, meaning "Ten-thousand Wealth", was 56 years of age. He was born and raised in

Johor Malaysia, near Singapore, but to make a living he had spent the better part of the last thirty years in Kudat. Up till a few years ago, he frequented islands around here, buying live fish for shipping to Hong Kong, Singapore and Taiwan, and in return selling diesel fuel and gasoline wholesale to the islands.

In fact, "Big Blue", the fishing boat with twelve wet tanks, used to belong to Mr. Ho for collection of live fish. He sold it to Abdul Latif at a bargain in down payment, with balance to be paid up indefinitely after Abdul used it to fish. Abdul, the current owner, is father of Anil and Pedy, the two fishermen I went out with. Now and then, maybe every two weeks, Mr. Ho, who was semi-retired, would come down to the jetty to pick up some free fish, perhaps as partial repayment for his boat. These days, the ocean had been depleted and some fishermen had converted their boats for divers or

Tip of Borneo / 婆羅洲最北端

angling sport fishermen. This very morning, Ho was taking home three large eels and some small fish to be cooked and fed to his dogs. And I was lucky to run into him.

Not only was Ho helpful in fixing and negotiating the boat charter for us, he said if I were to wait for him a couple days to settle his errands, he would even accompany me to the islands where he had many close friends from his years of business. At the same time, he could also be my interpreter and handle all the logistics. This was like a god-send for me; a one-stop clearing house for my next escapade. Above all, he was doing it for free!

I spent the next two days waiting for Ho by staying at a beach house half an hour away, at the Tip of Borneo. We took up three simple lodges just steps away from the sea, observing the sunset or the rainstorm moving across the ocean. Nearby, five minutes by car, was the literal Tip of Borneo. Coastal rocks jutting into the ocean saw waves pounding the coast as the tide surged and receded. They resembled several crocodiles, adults and babies, swimming out to sea.

A symbolic gate restricting visitors from going beyond for safety reasons marked this as the dividing point of the South China Sea and the Sulu Sea, to the west and east respectively. Another marker at the headland pointed to various capitals of the world, listing the distance from this point; Singapore being 1565 km, Bangkok 1925 km, Beijing 3654 km, London 11182, and so on and so forth. They all had measurements down to two decimal points. Hong Kong was 1731.07 km from the spot where I stood. To be exact, it was only 1731, as I had walked the 0.07 km toward the ocean beyond the marker.

Three lots from our beach lodge was Alvin's newly built seaside abode where he lived, with extension of four nice rooms for rent. These coastal beach front lots could only be allocated to local Bajau villagers, but were often leased out long-term to outside Malaysians or expatriate entrepreneurs. The lease was quite modest compared to one mansion on the headlands that listed in the Financial Times for a jaw-dropping 6,573,735 GBP.

Alvin was originally from nearby Kota Kinabalu, some three hours away by car. He is a professional diver and thus signed up to work in Macau for five years, performing at the House of Dancing Water of Dreams attached to the Melco group of casinos. After working five years in Macau, he had saved up enough money to return home and start his beach-front lodge here at the Tip of Borneo. His partner Ian ran the Blue Fin Dive Shop by the beach. Totally by coincidence, our CERS filmmaker Xavier, traveling with me on this trip, happened to be the director of the promotional film for the HODW, although he only filmed above water, while Alvin was a performer down below.

Divide of two seas / 南海與蘇祿海分界
Marker to capitals / 世界首都標記

Early morning on October 4, we drove back to Kudat and met up with Mr. Ho at the jetty. All papers were ready from the Marine Department, allowing us to board as passengers of the fishing boat. Freshwater and fuel tanks were filled, good for up to a week at sea. By 10am, we had set sail *bearing north, toward Banggi Island, largest of all islands in Malaysia, with an area of 440 square kilometers, a quarter larger than Penang Island to the north of the country or over five times that of Hong Kong Island. Yet it had only around 30,000 inhabitants spread out in many villages.*

We first stopped off at Batu Sirih Village on Balambangan Island, one of the satellite islands of Banggi where the East India Company established a trading post in 1773, negotiated by Alexander Dalrymple who made many sea charts, including around Hong Kong, the Philippines and Borneo. These islands today were all made into a nature park of Sabah State. Abdul, unrelated to boat owner, and Rambo came out in a speed boat to shuttle us to his village. Abdul was wearing a yellow

Sahara & HM exchange gifts / 莎哈拉與 HM 交換禮物

vest indicating that he was a park ranger for the reserve. Rambo carried a dark tan on his plumpish body with his name matching perfectly the persona of Sylvester Stallone today. The government has built a dozen or so cement houses for the village and Abdul was lucky enough to receive one, which he turned into a home-stay cottage. There we made our home for the night, sleeping on the floor with a thin pad.

The late season rainstorm came and went as I explored the two dozen or so homes along the coast. At least half a dozen homes were having a new boat built next to or under their houses. They were simple speed boats using basically plywood as material. I stopped by a neighbor's house as her loudspeaker was blasting some local tunes. Sahara's house was very clean, with many pictures of the family hung on her walls.

We sat at a cabana in her front yard to relax. Seeing that my Burmese longyi skirt was all wet from the rain, she suddenly brought out a beautiful sarong, perfectly ironed, and gave it to me as a gift. Such generosity to a total stranger and, given how little they had in their possession, was a very moving gesture. I quickly changed to the new sarong and asked Xavier to return to our fishing boat and bring over a CERS polo shirt and our cap as a return gift to Sahara.

While there were said to be many abalone along the coast, no one dared to dive for them. Man-eating crocodile frequented the water around here, especially where freshwater streams met sea water. The mangrove habitat these reptiles inhabited was shrinking, thus the crocs ranged further and began encroaching on human habitats. Rambo is an old friend of Mr. Ho. He showed me on his phone one of these large reptiles they had caught ten years ago.

The next day, we stopped at Karakit, the main port of Banggi Island where cars can take people to various villages around the island. Here was where the twice-a-day ferry from Kudat stops and turns around, a trip of around two hours across the bay. Five times a day, the call to prayer would come from the loudspeakers of the tall minaret of the yellow and green mosque by the jetty. At 5am, as well as with the evening call, it would trigger a massive chorus from the many stray dogs hanging around the village town.

It was at the jetty market that we bought a beautiful Emperor Red Snapper or, for Chinese, a San Du, meaning "Three Knife-Cuts", a coral reef fish with red and white stripes. It costs only 21 MYR (about USD $4) for the over-one-kilo beauty, with another nice garoupa thrown in. If bought in Hong Kong it would have easily fetch five times the price. Steamed at a local restaurant, it was delicious. We retired to our boat and slept on the front deck under a bright and shiny moon.

After a visit to the smaller island of Malawili described earlier, our last village stop was Sibogoh. From here, one could just barely see the silhouette of the two islands of Mangsee, belonging to Balabac in the Philippines. Out at sea by Sibogoh were many fish farms with sheds constructed on stilts. These were mainly for cultivation of sea cucumber, now a lucrative marine business, with harvest in dried form catering to the Asian market. The village houses, having over two hundred households, were all built on stilts, with their front facing the ocean and the back also against water and nearby mangrove forests.

Haji Tel is an old acquaintance and business associate of Mr. Ho. His title is evidence that he has been to Mecca as a pilgrim, despite that he was originally from Tawi Tawi in the southern tip of

Mindanao in the Philippines and married into a local family. With his speedboat as tender, he showed me his fish farm on floats where he keeps live fish. It had been passed down from Mr. Ho to him after Ho quit his live-fish business, and now it was only a third the size of the former float. We bought over a dozen abalone, two fish over one kilo each, and a live green lobster weighing 1.4 kilograms, all for a pittance. They were cooked by Tel's wife as our dinner.

As Mr. Ho was walking on the long board walk made of salvaged wooden planks with shophouses and homes fringing both sides, all the elders greeted him saying, "boss, boss", with a big smile. He had not returned to his former business hub for eight years and everyone was delighted to see him. He, for his own part, was extremely pleased that what used to be shabby shed homes were now colorfully painted new houses, some even resembling two-story village mansion.

"I feel that what I have brought over is not just new business, but improvement to the entire community," Ho related to me with a gratifying smile. No doubt he was an unintentional social entrepreneur, long before all these

Boat building at Batu Sirih /
峇都希利村裡的造船廠

Mosque at Karakit / 加拉吉的清真寺

Emperor Red Snapper / 皇帝紅鯛魚

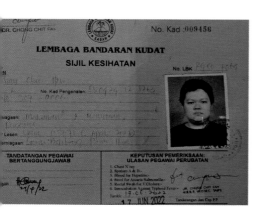

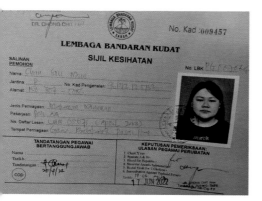

Chee How & Sou Man / 陳志效與陳秀文

packaged new-gen business measured by social impact index, CSR or ESG etc, became fashionable, in style and in vogue. For Ho, they were all cliché and passe. Impromptu efforts again trumped business modeling!

Back in Kudat town, we rushed again to my favorite noodles and roast meat restaurant operated by a Malaysian Chinese family. Seafood, despite being inexpensive, had been my only diet for days. Chan Chee How and Chan Sou Man, each with part of their name matching mine, were the brother and sister manning the shop. Any larger order, be it roast chicken, duck or pork, must be made in advance, as each day's delicacies were always sold out. One time, we were only allowed to have 10Rm (US2.5) of BBQ pork. Their chef would cook up our lobster head as bisque, with the large body served up as our lobster noodles.

Almost ninety percent of Kudat Town's shops were operated by Chinese. I pondered one for a moment at the main crossroad corner. It had a wall mural of an ancient Chinese junk, sailing off from the coast to arrive here in Malaysia. At the upper corner of the painting was the title "Overseas Chinese Moving South". It was a true account of the region's history, as I saw an older Chinese gentleman sitting inside sipping tea, while outside at the pedestrian corner a younger fellow was squatting and smoking a cigarette, just like the good old days.

After a ten-day sojourn, we drove off from Kudat, a frontiers of China's Nine Dash Line and a border with modern contention and a potential hot spot. I stopped at a row of roadside stalls selling colorful fruits and handicrafts, mainly woven bamboo and rattan wares. Here, I bought a golden custard apple, and a bunch of rambutan.

As I looked further at a small woven basket and a bundle of fully ripen baby banana, I asked the two young sisters, one around 8 the other maybe 12, whether I could just buy and taste one single banana. Surprisingly, the elder girl took down the entire bundle and passed it to me, saying, "Take it, it is free." Then the younger sibling followed and passed me the basket, "Here, take this too." What a nice finale to my first escapade to this distant land.

A place can be both strategic and beautiful, but above all it is the very nice people that count the most. I shall soon return.

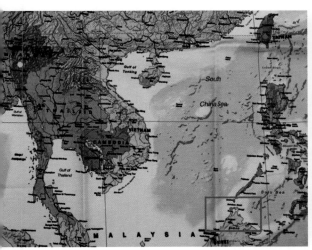

Location of North Borneo map / 北婆羅洲地圖位置

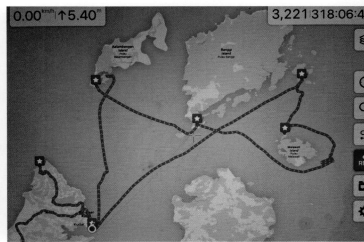

Route of Island Visit & potential future work /
島嶼參觀路線 & 未來可能的工作項目

在北婆羅洲跳島（下）

水上與陸地，還有水陸之間

如果不是因為我十天前先遇到這號人物，我根本無緣見識到「紅斑馬」海馬、沒機會認識費德老師與他的房東托頓。此人是我這趟北婆羅洲旅程中偶然相遇的關鍵人物。沒有他，就沒有漁船可租用、沒有島嶼可探索、沒有漁村可參觀。

那是十月一日的清晨六點。彼時彼刻，北京天安門廣場前正舉行升旗儀式，尤其當天是中華人民共和國的第七十三個國慶日而別具意義（儀式時間以日出的時辰來決定）。我凝望窗外的大海，三艘漁船從我眼前經過，應是出海捕魚一夜後，正往回家的方向前進。這些船的水線低，船頭也不高，看來應是滿載而歸。我決定衝到碼頭去，看看他們的漁獲，一方面也希望能認識這些漁船的船長或船主。

我記得前一天當我一抵達古達 (Kudat) 鎮時，我們在碼頭附近徘徊張望，希望能找到可供出租的船隻，完成我此行的目標——前往附近島嶼探索。但運氣欠佳，我幾乎找不到任何說英文的居民，身邊都是馬來人。鄰近的一些島嶼，都和我們曾經去過的菲律賓南端巴拉望島與巴拉巴克島相連。而婆羅洲北部屬於馬來西亞的島嶼，與菲律賓南部的巴拉望島嶼，再加上許多零星散布於中國南海的小島與環礁，都環繞在敏感的南沙群島。我一直很想好好了解這一區域的居民與周遭的環境。

碼頭上裝滿魚蝦蟹的籃子，擱置路旁，等著放上卡車；我再找機會和一位馬來人隨意攀談，看來他應該是其中一艘漁船的船主。他對我的提問一臉茫然，顯然雞同鴨講，他無從理解我想表達的意思。我轉過身，突然瞥見一位戴口罩、看似華人面孔的男性。我鼓起勇氣用幾句中文向他問候，希望他可以協助我翻譯幾句話，和這些馬來人溝通。

出乎我的意料，這位男士不只會說中文，而且還說得一口流利粵語。他是今年五十六歲的何萬發，顧名思義，即「萬」貫家財般「發」達富裕。何萬發在馬來西亞南部的柔佛州出生與成長，柔佛州離新加坡很近，僅一橋之隔。為了謀生，他過去三十年來大部分時間都待在古達鎮。直到幾年前，他還經常到附近的島嶼上尋找各種商機，他會購買活魚再運往香港、新加坡與台灣，回過頭再把柴油、汽油、天然氣等燃料批發賣給島嶼上的魚商。

事實上，我承租的那艘「大藍」漁船和漁船上的十二個水箱，原來都屬何萬發所有，是他用來收買活魚用的船。他後來把整艘船以低廉的價格賣給阿杜‧拉迪夫，讓阿杜先付一筆頭期款後，再按捕魚的收入，分期付款，彈性付清後續餘款。漁船主人阿杜的兩名兒子阿尼爾與斐狄，就是陪我出海的兩兄弟。大約每隔一兩個星期，半退休的何萬發會到碼頭來，拿些免費的現撈魚，或許可以視為償還漁船部分債務的回饋與默契吧。近日來，海洋資源

Unloading prawns / 卸蝦
House on stilt / 水上人家

日益枯竭，有些漁夫甚至已把原來的漁船改裝成適合水上休閒活動的裝備，提供潛水員或游釣運動出海，另闢謀生之道。今天上午，何萬發的收穫不少——三條大鱔魚和一些小魚——回去煮了可以餵他的狗。我也很幸運，能在這裡認識他。

何萬發不只幫我解決與協商許多租船事宜，他還告訴我，如果我能等他三兩天，讓他先把一些工作處理好，那他便可陪我到其他島嶼去找他的生意夥伴與老朋友。與此同時，他還可以當我的隨行翻譯，甚至一手包辦所有行程與住宿安排等大小瑣事。何萬發不但為我接下來的跳島出走提供「一條龍服務」，而且還完全免費！這對我來說，何止是天賜良機，根本機不可失啊！

接下來的兩天，為了等他把手頭上的任務處理完，我住到距離婆羅洲最頂端半小時路程的海濱房舍裡。我們投宿離大海只有數步之遙的旅舍三間獨立房子，就近觀望日落夕陽或在海上飄移不定的暴風雨。只要開車五分鐘的距離，就可以「腳踏實地」婆羅洲島的最尖端。沒入海中的岸邊岩石，日夜對著湧動的潮水與浪頭，送往迎來，拍打岸邊再退回大海。這些岩石的形狀，看起來仿若幾條大小鱷魚，載浮載沉地游向大海。

為確保訪客安全，這裡設置了一道象徵性的大門限制旅人出入，把西邊的南海與東邊蘇祿海之間的分界，做個標示。另一個在岬角的標誌，則是指向世界各個首都從當地出發的距離——新加坡離當地是 *1565* 公里、曼谷是 *1925* 公里、北京是 *3654* 公里、倫敦 *11182* 公里……。這些測量的距離精準到小數點後兩位數。香港和我腳下所立之地的距離，是 *1731.07* 公里。更準確地說，應該只有 *1731* 公里，因為我已朝向標識之外的海洋深處走了 *0.07* 公里。

和我們的海濱旅舍相隔三間房的不遠處，是艾爾文新蓋的海邊屋，他就住在那裡，另外加蓋了四間美輪美奐的房子，專出租給外人。這些海濱區域的房子地段，只分配給當地的巴瑤族居民，但實際上卻長期租給外來的馬來西亞人或外籍企業人士。和《金融時報》上報導的附近海岬豪宅相比，一套動輒高達 6,573,735 英鎊的天價租金，貴得令人瞠目結舌，看看這裡同樣是海岬大房，租金實在「甜美」得令人愛不釋手。

艾爾文來自沙巴首府亞庇 (Kota Kinabalu) 大城，從這裡開車去大約要三小時。艾爾文是個專業潛水員，因此而簽到在澳門工作五年的機會，在隸屬「新濠博亞」集團的澳門賭場——《水舞間》駐場表演。在澳門工作五年後，艾爾文存夠了錢，返回故鄉，在婆羅洲島海岬區的海岸最前線，蓋起自己的海濱旅館當房東；而他的夥伴伊安，也在海邊經營一家「藍鰭」潛水店。這趟旅程，「中國探險學會」的影片製作人李伯達 (Xavier) 和我同行，而他剛好曾是《水舞間》宣傳短片的導演，換句話說，當李伯達在水上拍片時，艾爾文正好在水底表演，這樣的機緣與巧合，實在太不可思議了。

十月四日一大清早，我們開車回到古達鎮，在碼頭與何萬發會合。所有必備文件都呈交海事部門，才能獲准以乘客身分登上漁船出海。飲用水與汽油箱都加滿滿了，足夠讓我們在海上漂流一週。

Turquoise water & beach / 碧綠的海水與海灘

Beach front lodge / 海濱小屋

上午十點左右，我們向北啟航，朝馬來西亞最大島邦宜 (Banggi) 島前進。邦宜島面積四百四十平方公里，比馬來西亞北部的檳城（檳榔嶼）大了四分之一，足足是香港島的五倍之大。邦宜島人口不多，居民約三萬人，分布於島內的許多村莊裡。

第一站，我們先停靠巴蘭邦岸 (Balambangan) 島的峇都希利 (Batu Sirih) 村，屬邦宜島的其中一個衛星島嶼；東印度公司曾在一七七三年時在此設立貿易站，由英國皇家首席水文師亞歷山大‧達爾林普爾 (Alexander Dalrymple) 完成交涉，他並標示與繪製許多海圖，包括香港周邊、菲律賓與婆羅洲等。直至今日，這些衛星島嶼都屬於馬來西亞沙巴州的自然公園。我們認識了另一個也叫阿杜的當地人（與之前的船主阿杜同名）與藍波，開著他們的快艇過來，把我們一行人送到他的村子裡。阿杜身穿黃色背心，顯然他是保護區的自然公園管理員。藍波一身黝黑結實的身形，他的名字恰好和美國好萊塢演員史特龍 (Sylvester Stallone) 在電影「藍波」裡所塑造的形象完全吻合。政府為了打造這座村子，蓋了十幾間水泥房；阿杜運氣真好，也被分配到一間，他把這房子轉為民宿小屋。我們就在這裡住一晚，鋪個薄睡墊，便席地而眠。

當我深入沿岸幾十戶人家去探索這塊區域時，後半段的雨季夾帶暴雨，下了幾場傾盆大雨。我發現其中至少有六戶家庭都有自己的新船，有的停放屋旁或房子底下。這些船看起來是簡單的快艇，基本材質是膠合板。我在一間房子前駐足停留，屋內的音響擴音器正在播放一些當地音樂。那是莎哈拉的房子，室內窗明几淨，牆上掛了好多家人的照片。

我們坐在莎哈拉前院的小木屋裡閒聊，身心放鬆。她看到我身上的緬甸長裙被雨淋濕

Fish drying / 晒魚

了，只見她一轉身便從屋子裡拿出一條熨燙得平整美麗的紗籠，喜孜孜地要送我當禮物。我之於她是個才剛認識的陌生人，但她卻對我如此慷慨付出，尤其想到她自己其實並不寬裕，我心裡滿是難以言喻的感動。我趕緊換上新的紗籠，請李伯達回到我們的漁船上，把一件「中國探險學會」的 polo 衫和我們的帽子拿來，當作回贈給莎哈拉的小禮物。

據說，沿海地區有不少鮑魚，但由於食人鱷魚經常出沒，人人聞之喪膽，尤其在淡水河域與海水交匯處，至今始終沒人敢潛水取鮑魚。這些爬行類動物喜歡棲息的紅樹林溼地，其實也不斷縮小，鱷魚的活動範圍越來越有限，只好把「魔抓」伸入人類的棲息地。藍波是何萬發的多年老友，他打開手機儲存的照片，讓我見識一下他們十年前抓到的其中一條巨大爬蟲。

Rambo with village kids / 藍波與村裡的小孩

隔天，我們停靠加拉吉 (Karakit)，那是邦宜島上最主要的港口，旅人可以在這裡搭車前往島上的各個村莊。從古達鎮出發的渡輪，每天兩班停靠這裡，並在這裡轉彎，搭一趟穿越海灣的行程需要兩小時左右。碼頭邊一間黃綠相間的清真寺，高聳的尖塔上一天五次按時放送穆斯林的祈禱聲。清晨五點與天色漸晚的祈禱召喚，總會引來遊蕩街上的流浪狗齊聲共鳴，仿若此起彼落的大合唱。

我們在碼頭市場上，買了一條漂亮的川紋笛鯛，魚身紅白條紋，中國人稱之為「三刀」，意思是「三條刀切」紋，屬珊瑚礁魚。這條超過一公斤的笛鯛物廉價美，只要馬幣二十一 (折合約四美元)，還另外附送一條肥美石斑魚。如果在香港，價格至少翻漲五倍。我們把鮮魚帶到當地一家餐廳以清蒸料理，大夥兒吃得食指大動，非常美味。飽餐一頓後，我們打道回船，就在「船前」明月光下，以甲板為榻，度過一夜。

結束上一篇內文提及的海角島嶼馬拉維利之行，我們的最後一站是到希波果 (Sibogoh) 島。從小島上可以勉強遙望屬菲律賓巴拉巴克 (Balabac) 市芒西 (Mangsee) 群島的其中兩島。希波果島的海面上，蓋了許多高架上的養魚場，以養殖海參為主。就目前的海產市場來看，海參肯定是有利可圖的火紅生意，一般以乾貨的方式供應亞洲的市場。島嶼上的漁村有兩百多戶人家都住在高腳屋裡，典

Crocodile caught / 被抓到鱷魚
Mosque at Karakit / 加拉吉島清真寺

型的水上人家；四面八方都是大海，以及附近的紅樹林。

哈吉特勒 (Haji Tel) 是何萬發的老友兼生意夥伴。光聽這名字的「哈吉」稱謂，已足以說明他是個曾到麥加完成朝覲的朝聖者；不過，他其實出身菲律賓民答那峨 (Mindanao) 島南端的塔威塔威 (Tawi Tawi) 省，因為娶了本地妻子而移居來此。他以快艇當交通船，向我展示他在浮筒上打造的養魚場。這是哈吉特勒從何萬發手中轉接過來的活魚生意，現在的養殖場面積只有過去的三分之一，範圍已縮減不少。我們買了十幾隻鮑魚、兩條各逾一公斤的魚，和一隻重達一點四公斤的青龍蝦，海鮮生猛，價格卻不高。這頓晚餐就由哈吉特勒的妻子為我們料理烹煮。

何萬發走在廢棄木板鋪成的長長走道上，兩旁是鱗次櫛比的店面與房子，所有的年長者都熱絡和他打招呼，稱他「老闆、老闆」。這裡曾是何萬發做生意的營業據點，他已八年沒回來這裡走動，大家久別重逢都喜眉笑眼；他自己也開心不已，尤其看到過去那些破舊不堪的棚屋現在都已煥然一新，改建成色彩繽紛的新房子，有些建築乍看

Houses of Sibogoh / 希波果島上的房子

Fish farm / 養魚場

下簡直就像雙層的鄉村大樓呢！

「我覺得自己不只把新的生意帶過來，而且還改善了整個社區。」何萬發回應我的提問時，臉上掛著心滿意足的笑容。沒錯，他早在新興商業模式開始流行所謂「企業社會責任」或「永續發展」等影響社會的指標前，便已是個自自然然實踐了社會責任的企業家。對何萬發來說，那些為了包裝企業形象而蔚為風潮的名詞，只是老套的話術，落伍了。不經意的及時努力，再次戰勝了商業模式！

回到古達鎮，我們再度衝到我最愛的烤肉麵店，一家由馬來西亞華人家庭經營的餐廳。雖然這裡的海鮮價格不高，但我已連續吃了好幾天只有海鮮的餐食。餐廳主人是陳志效與陳秀文兩兄妹，倆人的名字剛好湊合成我的名。要在這家餐廳訂餐，無論烤雞、烤鴨或烤豬肉，都必須提早預約，因為每一天的美味主食總是早早就賣完，供不應求。有一次我們來用餐時，因為沒有提早預約而只能點選馬幣十元（折合約二點五美元）的烤肉。餐廳主廚會把我們的龍蝦頭熬煮成湯底，把蝦肉料理成龍蝦麵。

Chinese migration mural / 中國移民壁畫　　　　Kudat Chinese restaurant / 古達中國餐廳

古達鎮上將近百分之九十的商店老闆都是華人。這現象的背後，其來有自。我在一家位於主要交叉路口角落的商店裡，駐足沉思了一會兒。這家店面的牆上，掛了幅壁畫，一艘古老的中國帆船，從中國沿海出發，前往馬來西亞這一頭。畫作上角寫著「華僑南遷」的標題。我相信這是當地歷史的真實故事，因為我在彼時當下，正好瞥見一位中國老派的長輩坐在店鋪裡喝茶，回過頭則看到一名年輕小伙子，蹲在人行道的轉彎處，神態自若地抽著菸；我滿眼看到的，都像時過境遷的往日好時光。

逗留了十天，我們從古達鎮開車離開——離開這個中國「九段線」的前哨地域，同時也是充滿爭議的邊界線與潛在的多事之地。我們在路邊一整排的攤販區停車，攤位上都是五彩繽紛的各種水果與手工藝品，以竹編與藤編為主。我買了一顆黃金果和一串紅毛丹。

我再仔細一瞧，一個小編織籃與一串熟透的小香蕉引起我的注意，我轉身詢問一個八歲、另一個約莫十二歲的兩姊妹，是否可以只買一根香蕉先嚐嚐味道。年紀較長的小姊姊竟把整串香蕉遞給我，並說：「拿去吧，免費給你！」出乎我的意料。接著，姊妹倆竟把籃子也送我。「這個也給你，你拿去。」第一次退隱到遙遠的海角島嶼，竟在旅程結束時，收獲如此令人喜出望外的結局。

這是一個兼具戰略熱區與迷人之地，但更令人念念不忘的，是這裡的暖暖人情味。我想，我很快會再回來。

Roadside vender / 路邊小販

金色三角洲

GOLDEN TRIANGLE

Chiangmai, Thailand – November 20, 2022

GOLDEN TRIANGLE
Connecting Myanmar to Laos through Thailand

Golden indeed, as I look at patches of harvested fields of rice, as well as other crops ripening in this late autumn season. In the past, the Golden Triangle's claim to fame however was not the lustrous rice crop so famous to Thailand, the largest exporter in the world. Gold referred to that white powdered substance that was as valuable as gold, or more so ounce for ounce.

Today, the opium is no more to be seen. What poppy fields there still are now not supposed to be seen. Instead, the region is now flush with other more beautiful, though not as profitable, growth, that of tourism and an array of agricultural products.

I have been in the area twice before, many years ago, to explore border regions. Now, I am scouting, sourcing, and prospecting, for the perfect location to set up "shop", hoping to connect our projects in upper Myanmar to those in northern Laos. It seems perfect to set up a base here in Thailand. After all, the country forms the baseline of the triangle, with the two flanks being Myanmar and Laos.

Not so far away is Yunnan Province, connected by the Mekong, where CERS has many sites and destinations within our project portfolio. I use the word "shop" and "portfolio", as CERS, with its current size, is gradually becoming more business-oriented and institutionalized, something I managed to defy and avoid for decades.

Flying into Chiangmai through Bangkok was easy, but staying at my friend Aarya's home was a curtain call on luxury before rougher days ahead. Still, an encore is awaiting when I return. A dinner was set at her other home high up on the hill above Chiangmai, surrounded by her beautiful farm and garden.

Joining us at dinner was the newly arrived US Consul General, among others. Lisa had just left her previous posting of a three-year stint in Beijing. In the past, her role here would have included dealing a lot with the US ATF bureau. Here, two of those letters, T for Tobacco and F for Firearms, have gone from undercover to irrelevant. Firearms are no longer prevalent, following the disbanding of the former remnants of Kuomintang army turned drug lords, who had operated from the hills near the border. Tobacco is shorthand for a variety of drugs, including marijuana, which is now legal in Thailand. We concentrate on the A for Alcohol, starting with champagne, and ending with wine and beer.

The following morning four of us start to hit the road in a pick-up truck. Aarya, despite her very busy schedule, offers to accompany me as my

Golden Triangle Map / 金色三角洲地圖
iPad route map / iPad 路線地圖

interpreter. Khun Dee, a retired tourism expert, will be my guide. Surprisingly there is a four-lane highway to Chiang Rai, though it winds through the undulating hills and valleys. After a couple hours, we switch to a side road heading due northeast toward Chiang Khong and the Mekong River. Khun Dee brings us to a roadside noodle shop no less delicious than the waiter-served fine dining at Aarya's famous Terra Restaurant adjacent to her home.

Chiang Khong used to be a quiet ferry crossing point between Laos and Thailand. Today, a newly constructed bridge spans the Mekong, with most traffic being huge trucks heading to or from China. I tried to locate the type of long tourist boats we had chartered in the past, hoping to modify one to become a mobile base for work up and down the Mekong River. It is a bit disappointing to find out that all such boats are over at Huay Xai on the Laos side, and we are not prepared to travel there, with the pandemic not yet fully under control.

We however saw locals crossing by smaller boats, landing on the Thai side at a small custom and immigration house. For border residents, a simple paper and I.D. serve as cross-border permits. At one secluded spot where some goats were grazing, I saw a young man get off his motorbike carrying a bottle of gasoline. He casually walked down to the bank of the river and boarded a tiny long-tail boat. Poling it to deeper water to start his engine, within a few minutes he was on the other side and up the Laos bank. Apparently, crossing river and between countries is like crossing the street for those living along the banks.

Looking up and down river from there, momentarily my memory brought me back to my explorations of the Mekong. I drank from the pristine water at its source in 2007. At its mouth in 2008, however, I only dared to dip my feet for a wash. Now I am here at its mid-point. Crossing time and space in the mind is as easy as crossing the river here, just as a rainbow descends on the bridge to bid us farewell to Chiang Khong.

An hour on, after some scenic driving with sporadic views of the river, we are in Chiang Saen. This is a small port city by the confluence of the Mekong and Kok River, right where the three countries, Thailand, Myanmar and Laos, meet. Here we made inquiries from the port executive officer regarding all the paperwork necessary to own and operate a boat on the Mekong. It can be done, though not easy.

Under his office and his nose were two large pleasure yachts, or cruisers I should call them. They were confiscated under his watch, being owned and operated by a dubious rich Chinese who was suspected of faking their registration on the Laos side and operated them as river casinos or brothels, or probably both. Vices always travel in good company, not alone.

Terra Restaurant/Bar / 泰拉餐廳酒吧

Ferry crossing on Thai side / 泰國這邊的渡輪

Long boat under new bridge / 新橋下的長船

In fact, this area used to go by only one law, that of the jungle. This has now been inherited by shady characters who lure innocent or naïve villagers to work in the casino and its peripheral service professions, offering high-paying but non-existent jobs. Many are diverted to operate phone and online scams that target victims throughout Asia. If they try to escape and run away, they may be sold to the next outfitter, like slaves. Many women end up in brothels. Kidnapping and human trafficking are prevalent in these border regions.

We stayed at the Imperial, one of the best hotels in the area, overlooking the Mekong. Architecture by the river took on both traditional and modern styles. Everything closes early here in Chiang Saen, though it is a tourist town with lots of tuk-tuk motorbikes. By 6pm, only a few riverside eateries remained open where "diners" sit on the floor over a mat. On a rainy day like today, that would not be a great choice.

Old-new houses by river / 河邊的新舊房屋

Chinese restaurant at Chiang Saen / 清盛縣的中國餐廳

After cruising back and forth, we found one suitable quiet restaurant. The entire place was run by young ladies. Somehow, the waitresses all acted as if they were mute and could not talk, as we pointed to our choices on the menu. In fact, they even avoided eye contact with us customers. Khun Dee told me that these are the luckier ones who escaped from Myanmar as refugees. Hired as illegal workers, they had better keep their mouth shut and look the other way. The local officials would also look the other way, for goodwill or for a little extra income.

Across the river on the Laos side are a few high-rise buildings all lit up, with one particularly beautiful one with neon changing colors. It is shaped somewhat like a poppy flower on the top. This is the Kings Romans Casino with its surrounding hotels, operated by an ex-triad boss. Just a month ago, newspaper reported this as being a center for brothels, online scam calling center, trafficking humans, animal parts and drugs. The huge plot of land reportedly has a 99-year lease from the Laos government. The Thais call this Laos Vegas, though it is not star-studded with celebrity performers. Our future base should offer something more refreshing and positive to balance this heinous and notorious place.

Next stop in the morning is an hour or so away - Mae Sai, a border town. Across a small stream is Tachileik of Myanmar. In the past during better

Kings Romans Casino / 羅馬大王賭場
Bridge between Thailand & Laos / 泰國接寮國大橋

days, this was a very busy crossing point between the two neighbor countries. Today, the border has been closed for almost three years. A lone soldier stands guard at a metal shed on the Thai side, making sure no one wades across the stream from the other side.

When asked, he admits to catching one or two people trying to sneak through each month. But for those just wading into the river to catch fish, or pretending to fish, he can do little unless they step on shore. With less than five meters between the two countries where the guard post is, houses on both sides are within talking, not even shouting, distance. I would not be surprised if young men and women cast loving eyes upon each other across the border.

At a line of shops along the border many shop owners can speak Mandarin. Not a few attest that their ancestors are from Yunnan of China. We stop by a large tea and coffee café to have a drink. It also sells porcelain and ceramic deity statues, all obviously made in China. It is apparent that there is a sizable population of Chinese origin in the region.

Under normal circumstances, I would have crossed the border bridge, had lunch in Myanmar and been back for dinner on the Thai side. But it is not to be, and we drive on along some windy mountain roads, climbing to a high ridge overseeing far-off mountains standing in ranks into the distance. We are on our way to visit Mae Salong, the name of a hero, or a renegade, depending on which side of the fence you sit.

This is the hilltop encampment of a remnant Kuomintang army that retreated from Yunnan into

Tachileik shop / 大其力城裡的商店

this mountain enclave. The history of the 93rd Division is famous and could fill an entire book. To describe it in one short paragraph does no justice, but these days there is little justice in the world. For more details, be they interpreted by the left or the right, plenty can be Googled or found in Wikipedia. My personal encounter however, will follow. Brief, but evolutionary.

The 93rd Division first fought the Japanese, both in China and then as an expeditionary force in Burma. Then came the Civil War after Japan surrendered. Driven out of Yunnan by the PLA, the 93rd, including many of their family members, retreated into northern Thailand along the Burma borderland with over 17,000 troops. They directed occasional raids into the young People's Republic of China, later fought the Burmese regular army and won, and successfully deterred the Thai army from driving them away. The UN stepped in and batches of soldiers were repatriated to Taiwan. The remaining ones ended up helping the Thai government eradicate Communist guerillas in the north and as a result were rewarded with Thai residency. Some heavily armed camps ended up becoming opium growers and drug lords, like the infamous Khun Sa of the Golden Triangle, until they were finally pacified and turned into farmers in their former mountain citadel.

We choose the best restaurant in town at Mae Salong to have lunch. The name of the place escapes me, but the music lingers on; repeat after repeat of the most popular song by Taiwan singer Theresa Teng, "The Moon Represents My Heart" throughout my hour of lunch. So now it is known among us as Theresa Forever Restaurant.

The restaurant premises belongs to the former renegade General Duan Xiwen of the 93rd Division.

There is a huge memorial gate next door leading to his grave up the hill. Apparently, he is still revered by his soldiers and even among descendants of the 93rd. Many of them have turned to growing tea in this hilltop area with mist and fog much of the year. Some of the best tea has been transplanted from Taiwan.

As we leave the restaurant, we ask the waiters where is a good place to buy some tea. They tell us the name of one larger shop to the left of the road. Soon we pull up and stop at Zhu Huiqin's tea shop. It is probably the largest of all tea shops in this hilltop town.

My encounter with Zhu, more personal and less dramatic, nonetheless is perhaps representative of the state of mind and being of descendants of the 93rd. Zhu is an older lady of 74, and has lost most of her teeth, to which I too can relate. She keeps offering to brew us some tea to try, while I am busy checking on her huge variety of vacuum-packed tea below and over the back of the counter. She is fluent in Mandarin Chinese and we quickly

Hill top Mae Salong Village / 山頂上的美斯樂鎮　　　　General Duan's Mausoleum Gate / 段希文將軍的陵墓門

strike up a conversation. Born in 1948 in Teng Chong of Yunnan bordering Myanmar, she came with her parents as a child together with the army when they retreated from Yunnan into the Golden Triangle in the early 1950s. Since the tension has subsided, she has visited her home in Yunnan a few times.

She brags about her tea, some of which are varieties from the Taiwan Alishan region. There are also old plantation trees that she attests to being picked only once every two years, as well as other first flush selections. I choose indiscriminately, as I know little about tea, selecting the most colorfully packaged ones. Zhu seems particularly proud that she is a descendent of the KMT army, pointing to a roadside tablet marking that pertains to the 93rd Division.

Zhu insists on opening a new pack to brew for us, despite there being many opened packs on her tea-serving counter. She teaches me that the longer cup in the tea service, which is turned up-side-

Zhu with tea / 朱惠琴與茶葉　　　　Zhu brewing tea / 朱惠琴正在沖泡茶　Mae Salong tea shop / 美斯樂的茶葉店

down inside the shorter teacup, is for lifting to the nose and smelling the fragrance of tea while sipping the brew. Something novel to me, despite drinking tea all my life.

As we chat, we became more like old acquaintances, and she ends up giving me a huge discount on the tea I purchase, as well as throwing in a couple more varieties as gifts. Apparently, she is not that eager on making a living out of her merchandise and seems ready to get rid of her stock and close shop, since none of her children would like to continue with this trade. I have never bought so much tea in my entire life.

When she finds out that I am a writer, Zhu quickly picks up her small handbag, insisting on showing me one of her premises that she thinks will be perfect as a writer's retreat. She leaves her shop wide open to the street, and simply walks off and into our truck. Some four hundred meters away down the hill is an area designated as a memorial park for the 93rd Division. A modern hostel there is supposedly funded by Taiwan.

Beyond is a line-up of small, connected shops with shuttered doors under lock. Zhu point to ones that belong to her, but I decline her offer to open up the place, as the location is not what I would consider much of a retreat. Zhu says that she owns other land, including one spot where her husband, a former officer of the 93rd, is buried. I have to tell the enthusiastic lady that time is running out and we must move on, after dropping her at her tea shop. Surprisingly, a few tourists are already in her shop, wondering where the owner had gone.

Our drive drops down to the plains before going through some beautiful limestone hills around Chiang Rai and upstream along the Kok River. Peaceful as the area might look, it reminds me that, for 18 days in 2018, the area was the setting for a real-life drama that caught the attention of the entire world, with network news broadcasting every day from this remote location.

It was then that the Wild Boar Football Team of twelve young boys and their coach were caught inside Tham Luang Cave when the flooded river blocked their exit. It took a week for cave divers to verify that they were still alive, although not well. More than another week passed before they were gradually taken out by the rescue team in dives to safety. The boys had to be sedated in order to bring them out. Two Thai Navy divers died during the early search, and it was a UK and Australian professional dive team that finally succeeded in coordinating the final rescue.

Elon Musk's offer to help with a state-of-the-art submersible became a side-bar distraction and mockery of an elongated ego. Perhaps, in the future, our more modest CERS caving team from Yunnan can also come and explore Tham Luang Cave, now made famous by one of the most successful rescues in modern times.

That however is for the future. For the moment, my mind is set on returning to Chiang Mai and Vana Som, the lovely villa home of my friend Aarya. An encore of fine Thai cuisine with a touch of natural farm produce, not to mention a brass hot tub with art deco fixtures, are all awaiting.

Vana Som villa / 瓦納索姆別墅

金色三角洲

取道泰國，連結緬甸至寮國

確實金色無誤，尤其在深秋時分凝視眼前一片收割的稻田與其他成熟的農作物。只是，在過去，所謂「金三角」的盛名，指的不是世界最大稻米出口國所產出的晶瑩剔透泰國米——「金」光閃閃的光芒，說的是白色粉末的東西，和黃金一樣價值連城，有些甚至比黃金更高價。

今天，我們已經看不到任何鴉片了。現在觸目所及的罌粟田，其實也「不該」被看見。取而代之的，是更妊紫嫣紅、盛開怒放的其他農作物；利潤或許不高，但卻與觀光產業相關。

許多年前，我曾兩度來此探索邊界境地。現在，我正在這裡進行探勘、考察，竭盡所能尋找一個最理想的「商店」定點，希望能藉此把我們在緬北的計畫與寮國北部的工作結合起來，更妥善地「經營」。我的想法是，若能在泰國建立一個結合兩國的據點，那就太完美了。畢竟，以泰國的地理位置來說，也正好是一個三角形的基礎線——緬甸與寮國各占左右兩邊。

離此不遠處，是與湄公河相連的雲南省，這是「中國探險學會」設置許多結合工作計畫的據點與目的地。你或許已注意到我使用「商店」與「經營」的商業詞彙，那其實

是面對「中國探險學會」的組織規模化過程中，我這十幾年來亟欲抗拒與避開、卻又不得不面對的實況——逐步走向商業化與制度化的方向。

取道曼谷、飛往清邁，一路順暢；原以為借宿友人阿雅 (Aarya) 家是體驗苦日子前最後的奢華享受。出乎意料的是，我竟在這趟回程時迎來加碼版的享樂。我受邀到阿雅清邁山上的另一個家，在她美麗的農場與花園裡，享用一頓氛圍迷人的晚餐。

和我們一起享用晚餐的賓客中，包括新就任的美國領事館大使麗莎。她剛離開之前在北京待了三年的工作崗位。過去，麗莎在這裡要扮演的角色包括與「美國菸酒槍炮及爆裂物管理局」（簡稱 ATF) 居間協調與交涉許多事務。其中的英文字母「T」代表「菸草」，而「A」指的是「槍砲」；只不過，這些原來要暗地裡進行的重要管制，已演變成無關緊要的業務，因為自國民黨殘餘分子解散後，孤軍已搖身一變成為活躍邊境山區的毒梟，槍砲已不普遍。至於菸草，那是包括大麻等各種毒品的簡稱，不過，這在泰國也已合法化了。既然如此，那我們就全神貫注把「A」字母重新定義成英文的「酒精」(Alcohol) 吧——從香檳開始，以紅酒和啤酒結束，賓主盡歡。

隔天早上，我們四人坐上皮卡車上路。日理萬機的阿雅，排除

Farm on hilltop / 山頂上的農場
Small boat across Mekong / 橫跨湄公河的小船

萬難，不僅全程陪伴我，也樂於當我的隨行翻譯。退休的旅遊專家坤迪 (Khun Dee) 則是我此行的嚮導。我們開往清萊的高速公路雖然沿著丘陵與山谷中蜿蜒前進，但四線道的路寬，令我無比驚訝。幾個小時後，我們逐漸走上一條小路，朝東北方向的清孔 (Chiang Khong) 縣與湄公河走去。嚮導坤迪帶我們到一家路邊的麵店用餐，其美味絲毫不亞於阿雅家旁著名的泰拉餐廳 (Terra Restaurant) 所提供的精緻美食。

過去，清孔縣是連結寮國與泰國之間一個冷清的渡輪碼頭。今時不同往日，這裡已新建一座大橋，橫跨湄公河，車水馬龍，大部分交通以往來中國的大卡車為主。我到處尋找曾經租用過、專載遊客的那種長型船，期待能改裝一艘，當成我們在湄公河上下游工作時的移動式據點。遺憾的是，類似的遊船都在寮國那一頭的會晒 (Huay Xai)，但這一次因為那裡的新冠疫情尚未趨緩，所以此行並不打算過去。

不過，我們倒是發現當地人大多以小船過河，再到泰國邊境上岸；岸邊設有規模不大的海關與移民關口。對於邊境居民來說，出入只需出示一張文件與身分證即可。我在一旁的僻靜角落，瞥見一小群山羊低頭吃草，附近一名年輕人緩緩從機車下來，手上拎著一瓶汽油。只見他悠悠然走到河岸邊，上了一艘小型長尾船。然後，他把小船划到較深的水域，啟動引擎，幾分鐘內便輕鬆抵達對岸的寮國邊境內，雖然是另一個國界，但看來對生活在兩岸邊際的人來說，在兩國之間遊走進出，就像過一條馬路般，稀鬆平常。

在河岸邊環顧與凝視周遭時，頃刻間，我想起許多年前，我們前往湄公河的探源過程與記憶。二○○七年，我在湄公河的源頭，喝了口純淨甘醇的水。然後，才相隔一年，

Boat on Mekong / 湄公河上的船隻

Storm over Golden Triangle /
金色三角洲上的風暴
Border crossing Thailand into Myanmar /
泰國緬甸邊境

二〇〇八年當我再到河口時，我只敢把腳浸入水中搓洗兩下。而今，我又來到湄公河的中心點。在心中跨越時間與空間是一件不費吹灰之力的事，仿若在這裡渡河般輕而易舉，抬眼一看，橋上正好一道彩虹懸掛空中，似乎有意送別我們離開清孔縣。

一小時車程後，經過一些山清水秀的風貌與路段，我們終於抵達清盛縣。這是個港口小城，位於湄公河與沱江交匯處，就在泰緬寮的三國交界處。我們順道在此向港口官員詢問「在湄公河上擁有船隻」的可行性與必備文件。雖然可行，但看來並不容易。

我在這名官員的辦公室外發現兩艘大遊艇，或許說它是軍艦比較適切。這兩艘遊艇是在他手中被扣押的，船主是名中國富豪，疑似在寮國偽造登記證，把大船當成河上賭場或妓院，甚至可能兩者兼具，進行「多角經營」。無雙不成惡？傷風敗俗的惡習，總是喜歡勾肩搭背，結伴而行。

其實，這區域向來只有一套法令──叢林法則。但現在這些法條已被黑白兩道、背景複雜的人物操控，他們利誘純樸天真的村民投入賭場與周邊服務業的工作，口頭允諾提供高薪，但事實上卻是不存在的工作。許多人被拐入電話與網路的詐騙行列，整個亞洲都是他們設定的詐騙對象。那些試圖逃跑卻又被抓回來的人，可能會像奴隸般，被賣給另一個犯罪集團；許多女性就這樣淪落

到妓院裡。在這邊境區域，綁架與人口販賣是司空見慣的事，屢見不鮮。

我們下榻當地的帝國飯店，那是當地其中一家最好的飯店，景觀美極了，還可俯瞰湄公河。河岸邊結合了傳統與現代風格的建築，非常獨特。雖然清盛縣是個滿街嘟嘟車的觀光城市，但這裡的商店早早便打烊休息。一到傍晚六點，只剩幾家河邊小餐館還在營業，一些「用餐人」在墊子上席地而坐。不過，像今天這斜風細雨的狀況，坐地上用餐似乎不是個理想的選擇。

來回幾趟遊走後，我們找到一家安靜的餐廳。整間餐廳都由年輕女士接待與服務，當我們指著菜單點餐時，所有女服務員都表現得好像啞巴似的，不言不語，甚至避開與我們眼神接觸。坤迪告訴我，這些女生算是比較幸運，可以以難民身分逃離緬甸。她們屬非法勞工，所以，和客戶之間最好閉上嘴巴，保持距離，以策安全。面對此事，當地執法人員無論是為了善意或為自己掙點額外收入，他們並未強制取締，睜隻眼、閉隻眼，視而不見。

河對岸的寮國那一頭，幾棟高樓建築的通明燈火在黑夜中顯得特別亮眼，其中一座還有閃爍的霓虹燈，光芒四射。這座建築高樓的外型獨特霸氣，仿如高樓頂端開了一朵罌粟花。那是羅馬大王賭場與其周邊的飯店，背後的經營大權掌握在從事販毒等非法活

Imperial overlooking Mekong /
從帝國飯店俯瞰湄公河
General teahouse / 段將軍茶店

Blue border guardhouse by stream /
溪邊的藍色邊境警衛室

動的中國祕密組織「三合會」前老闆手中。一個月前，報紙才大肆報導過此區已淪為妓院、網路詐騙電話中心、人口、動物器官與毒品販賣等「罪大惡極」集中地。根據報導，這塊大面積的土地已由寮國政府以九十九年租約出租。雖然賭場裡少了星光熠熠的名人演出，但泰國人習慣稱此為寮國的拉斯維加斯。我們「中國探險學會」的未來據點，是不是應該推動一些更「耳目一新」、有益身心健康的計畫來平衡一下這地方的惡名昭彰呢？

我們隔日上午出發往下一站，行車大約一小時，抵達與緬甸的大其力城接壤的邊境小城——美塞。過去，當世局安穩時，這是兩國間繁忙的過境之地，人車川流不息，往來不斷。可惜昨是今非，邊境已關閉近三年。泰國那一側的鐵皮哨站裡，留下孤單的士兵站崗守護，確保沒有非法涉水入境者。

當我們問這位士兵時，他坦承平均每一個月都會抓到一兩個試圖非法逾越邊境的偷渡客。不過，如果他們只是蹲在水中捕魚或假裝「混水摸魚」，他也莫可奈何，力有未「逮」，除非他們上岸。邊界哨站的位置，就在兩國之間不到五公尺距離，近到不必大聲喊叫便可就近對話，清晰可聞。倘若「有情人」各守一邊國界，以眉目傳情或互訴愛意，我可一點也不會驚訝。

邊境區域的一排商店裡，大部分店家都能說華語。其中不少人聲

稱自己的祖先來自中國雲南。我們走進一家規模比較大的咖啡館。這家咖啡館還販售瓷器與陶瓷神像，顯然都是中國製造。這區域祖籍中國的人口，看來不少。

過去一般情況下，我應該只需穿越邊界橋梁，到緬甸那邊吃中餐，然後再返回泰國這裡吃晚餐。但實情並非如此。我們沿著一條蜿蜒的山路，幾番曲折爬行到高聳的山脊，遙望遠方層巒群山。我們這一路的目的地是參訪美斯樂 (Mae Salong)，一個對「英雄與叛徒」兼容並蓄之地，亦邪亦正，就看你從哪個角度來檢視。

這個山頂營區，聚集了一支從雲南逃離共產黨、撤退來此的國民黨孤軍與後裔。這群被稱為國民黨

HM & border guard / HM 與邊境警衛

93 師官兵的故事，世人耳熟能詳，可以洋洋灑灑寫成一本書。如此沉重的歷史，若只以簡短一兩段話來敘述，未免過於簡化，也有失公允；不過，話說回來，這世上真正公義的事，本來就少見。關於這段歷史的細節，無論是左派敘述或右派表述，無論維基百科或谷歌搜尋，都可以找到大量的相關內容。至於我個人的進階版際遇，容我後續簡述。

國民黨第 93 師最初先在中國境內與緬甸，以遠征軍身分和日本對抗。日本投降後，內戰接踵爆發。被解放軍趕出雲南後，第 93 師的官兵帶著自己的家人，浩浩蕩蕩的一萬七千孤軍隊伍，沿著緬甸邊境，撤退到泰北。他們偶爾會襲擊剛成立不久的中華人民共和國，後來因成功擊退緬甸正規軍而為自己立下汗馬功勞，於是，泰國軍隊便手下留情，不把這批暫居於此的孤軍趕走。當聯合國介入後，成批軍官被遣送回台灣，剩下的士兵幫助泰國政府剿除北部的共產黨游擊隊，因勞苦功高而取得泰國居留權。有些武裝全備的軍防重地最終淪為鴉片種植者與毒梟的基地，譬如金三角的一代毒王，惡名昭彰的坤沙 (Khun Sa)，便是一例。一直到毒品輝煌的高峰期過了，農民重返他們的農地，棄鴉片，改種田。

我們挑了美斯樂鎮上最好的一家餐廳享用午餐。餐廳的名我早已不復記憶，但餐廳播放的音樂卻餘音繞梁，不斷迴盪我耳邊；吃午餐的那一小時內，台灣歌手鄧麗君膾炙人口的＜月亮代表我的心＞，唱了一遍又一遍。那家餐廳至今仍是我們心目中永遠的鄧麗君餐廳。

這餐廳原屬於國民黨第 93 師的前將軍段希文的房子。一旁有個巨大的紀念門，可以通

往山上他的墳墓。顯而易見，他仍備受部屬士兵、甚至 93 師後代的敬重。許多遺孤的下一代，轉而在這常年濃霧籠罩的山頂種植茶葉。其中有些頂級的茶葉，其實是從台灣移植過來的。

當我們準備離開餐廳時，我們詢問服務員附近可有買茶的地方。他們指向路旁左邊一家大型商店，我們很快便在朱惠琴的茶葉店門口停車，這確實是山頂小鎮上最大的一家茶葉店。

和朱惠琴相識，是個比較私人、平和含蓄的過程，但或許能代表 93 師孤軍後裔的生活與心態。朱惠琴是個七十四歲老婦，牙齒幾乎掉光了，關於「沒齒難忘」的體驗我是感同身受的。她不斷要我們泡些茶來試喝，而我卻忙著查看她櫃檯下方與後方一大批真空包裝的茶葉。朱惠琴說得一口流利普通話，我們很快就聊開了，倆人相談甚歡。她一九四八年在雲南騰衝出生，騰衝與緬甸接壤，離邊界不遠；一九五〇年代初期，國民黨軍隊從雲南撤退到金三角地區時，幼年的朱惠琴跟著父母一起到此，落地生根。政治對立的緊張局勢趨緩後，她曾返回雲南老家好幾次。

她對自己的茶葉讚不絕口，其中一些茶種是來自台灣阿里山的好茶。這裡還有些老茶樹，她每兩年才採擷一次，當然也有其他春摘茶可供選擇。我對茶葉所知不多，於是，隨意挑了幾包包裝鮮豔的茶葉。朱惠琴似乎對自己身為國民黨孤軍後代的身分與有榮

Mae Salong street venders / 美樂斯鎮上的小販們
Child vender / 小孩攤販

焉，她指著路邊一塊標示第 93 師相關的石牌，驕傲地表明自己的身分。

雖然桌上已開了好幾包給客人試喝的茶包，朱惠琴還是堅持要開一包新茶，請我們喝好茶。她特別教我，茶具有個上下顛倒放置在小茶杯裡的長杯，是聞香杯，喝茶時拿到鼻子前聞聞茶香。我雖然喝茶也喝了一輩子，但這對我來說還是挺新鮮的經歷。

話匣子一開，我們聊得投機，彷彿一見如故，於是，結帳時特別給了我大優惠，還額外送我幾包不同品種的茶葉當禮物。看來她其實志不在賣茶，也無需靠經營茶葉維生，反倒比較想盡早把既有的存貨賣完，結束生意，因為她的孩子們都不樂見她繼續工作。我滿載而歸，這輩子恐怕還沒買過那麼多茶葉。

當朱惠琴發現我是個作家時，她二話不說，趕緊拎起手提包，堅持要帶我去看個地方，她認為那絕對是個適合作家修身養性的好所在。她迫不及待，連店門都顧不得關起來，便坐上我們的卡車。下山約四百公尺之處，眼前出現一個專為 93 師而設的紀念公園。公園內有個現代化的宿舍，極有可能由台灣資助蓋建。

後方是櫛比鱗次的一排小店面，但大門深鎖。朱惠琴指著其中一間她的房舍，表示可以開放讓我使用，但我婉拒她的好意，因為那不是我心目中的隱居地。朱惠琴還告訴我，她仍有其他土地，包括其中一個埋葬前 93 師軍官丈夫的地方。我依舊婉拒這位熱情的女士，不得不提醒她時間不多，我們還必須繼續前行的旅程，說罷便把她送回茶店。一到茶店門口，驚訝發現已有好幾位找不到店主人的遊客，好奇張望，等著要買茶。

我們從高處逐漸下山，往平原走去，然後再穿越清萊周遭迷人的石灰岩山丘，沿著泰國的郭河逆流而上。這區域令人感覺寧謐清新，但在幽靜景觀的背後，卻令人忍不住想起二○一八年，引起全球矚目的十八天現實生活受困劇的背景，就在這裡上演，全球媒體的每日焦點都轉移到這個偏遠地區來追蹤報導。

當時，十二名年輕男孩組成的野豬足球隊和他們的教練因突然暴漲的溪流堵住洞窟出口，而受困「睡美人」(Tham Luang Cave) 洞窟。洞穴潛水員耗費一週才證實這群受困的隊員儘管身體虛弱，但都還活著。再過一個多星期，他們才被救援隊一一帶離洞窟，潛入安全區域。為了把這些孩子們帶出來，救援隊必須讓他們服用麻醉劑令到他們昏迷不醒人事。兩名泰國海軍潛水員在最初的搜尋過程中意外死亡，最終由英國與澳洲的專業潛水隊成功協調並完成最後階段的救援工作。

伊隆・馬斯克 (Elon Musk) 曾提議要用最先進的潛水器來協助救援，這無疑是擾亂民心又拙劣的「伊隆式」自我膨脹手法。或許將來我們這支來自雲南，謙遜又低調的「中國探險學會」也可以來探索這「睡美人」洞窟——這個在現代社會中最成功的救援而名聞天下的洞窟。

不過，那終究是未來的事。至於當下，我歸心似箭，只想回到清邁，回到瓦納索姆別墅——我朋友阿雅的可愛好宅。我要在那裡再次品嘗充滿天然食材風味的精緻泰式料理，更別提那充滿藝術裝飾的銅製熱水浴缸了……它們都在熱烈召喚我。

海岸城鎮奇遇記（第一章　廣西篇）

COASTAL ESCAPADE (Part I Guangxi)

Guangxi, Guangdong, Fujian, Zhejiang – Dec 2022 to Jan 2023

COASTAL ESCAPADE (Part 1 Guangxi)
Exploring fishing villages and ports

It was exactly ten years ago in December 2012 that I first arrived at Border Sign Post Number One, put here during the Qing Dynasty in 1890 to mark the beginning of China's land border, which stretches over 22,000 kilometers from this spot. On that previous trip, we began our journey inland, studying the land border of China with Vietnam, then Laos and finally with Myanmar as we ended our exploration on Yunnan's western border, having covered only a fraction of China's land border.

Border Sign Post Number One is also where China's long seacoast begins, extending for 18,000 kilometers from here. This time, our sojourn will go east, following China's long coastline to visit large and small fishing villages and ports, as well as a few inland enclaves not far from the coast. Given time constraints, my intention is to stop with Shanghai, perhaps covering a third of China's coastline.

At the time when Sign Post Number One was set up, Qin Zhou County, now belonging to Guangxi Province, was still under the jurisdiction of Guangdong. China was then surrounded by Western powers, each taking extra-territorial rights among its inland and coastal cities. The French dominated China's postal service, while the British took over many of China's custom houses, taking in cash as war indemnity payments by the Chinese government. The French, with its colony encompassing Vietnam and much of Laos, took over not only political, economic and maritime privileges, but extended its religious encroachment as well. The Sino-French War which ended in 1883 provided additional concessions to the winner, including the right to send their missionaries from the coast to China's heartland. One such mission got even into Tibet.

The French Catholic church here near the border with Vietnam at Shan De Village was first built in 1850 at Ju Shan (Bamboo Mountain), but was further expanded and consolidated after the French won the War in 1883. The inhabitants of these nearby villages are of the Jing nationality, a minority of China with less than thirty thousand people. On the Vietnamese side just across the bay separating the two countries, the Jing population is much larger, totaling 86% of the country's people, some 75 million in all, and dominating the countries government and business. On China's side, however, they are mainly traditional fisherman, living along the coastal border.

In the beginning, a single French priest was able to convert 28 households with only 132 converts. As the church expanded in size, a convent was

Along coast to Guangxi / 廣東往廣西沿海
Sign Post Number 1 / 一號界碑

added with ten sisters living in it. After the Communist took over all of China in 1952, some thirty households with over two hundred converts left the country and entered Vietnam permanently. Church activity was not resumed until 1984, almost a decade after the Cultural Revolution ended. By the 1990s, there were a total of 360 Catholic converts. Today, the church can hold around 200 people. While no priest is residing at the church today, the local elders organize functions during special religious days like Easter and Christmas, as well as Sunday prayer groups.

Jin Tan, meaning Golden Beach, is also populated by the Jing nationality. From a former obscure fishing village, it has now become a tourist paradise with many free independent travelers staying at local boutique or larger hotels along the sandy beach. We choose one small hotel right beside the sand to stay and park our camper van so I can sit to observe the tidal changes from low to high, becoming surf that pounds the coastal cement breaker then washes up to where I sit. The pandemic provided a huge bargain, as each room with balcony view costs a meager 120 RMB.

Local boats with a tilted flat bow are at anchor, but go out to sea to set nets each morning. Formerly built with bamboo or wood, modern materials are now available, as they have converted the lower half of the boats to use foam in order to provide better floatation. Further out at sea, they can bring back a good catch of green or blue crab, as well as near-coast fish of all types. Once the tide goes out, the long sand and mud flats also yield many types of shell fish. A local term gan hai becomes a popular attraction, meaning "chasing the sea" as people rush out on foot following the receding ocean to collect all types of shells and marine life coming out from its hide, just like egrets and other shore birds would do.

Enjoying tidal rhythm / 欣賞潮汐的韻律

Among less than 30,000 Jing nationality in China, 67-years-old Su Chunfa has a special place. He was chosen as a rare member among China's non-material heritage holders, being considered the national artist of the special single-string instrument of the Jing nationality. Today, he directs an orchestra troupe with sixteen members performing on this unique instrument, traveling the country on invitation as well as appearing on TV and the internet.

But Su is more than that, being multi-talented, including serving other civilian duties. In the 1960s, he was an electronics engineer and made two-way radios for the fishing fleet. Today, he is head of the local village volunteer fire brigade and is called upon whenever there is a fire to put out, riding his all-terrain vehicle to the scene of emergency.

Totally by coincidence, we run into him sitting watch at Golden Beach. Looking out at sea and patrolling the coast with a motorcycle, Su is heading a unit on lookout for smuggling, generally of

Bamboo boat with foam / 加裝保麗龍的竹船

Wood boat with foam base / 保麗龍基底的木船

small commercial items like cigarettes, traditional medicinal herbs, seafood and other sundry products between Vietnam and China. Nearby Wanwei Island is barely ten to fifteen minutes boat ride away from Vietnam.

As an entrepreneur, he owns three fishing boats which he charters out to fishermen in return for a fee plus part of their catch. Moving into wholesale fishery, at its height his daily purchase of seafood reach over a ton of fish and he has them shipped to nearby provinces. But due to the marine conservation policy of China, each year between May and September, there are now three to four months when off-shore fishing is prohibited. During that time, each fishing boat will receive compensation of 7,000 RMB.

The prolific Su suggested we visit, just a few blocks away, one of four Ha Temples of the Jing people. These are traditional centers of worship of the sea god for the Jing, for the blessing of calm waters when at sea. Including those in Vietnam, there are only twelve such temples in existence. Thus, the Jing in China, though small in number, are considered a bearer of the ancient tradition of this ethnic group.

We visit one other fishing port of Guangxi, San Lang Wan, also in Qin Zhou, before entering Guangdong. The bay has undergone much renovation to becoming a recreational park. Former fishing village houses have now been replaced by three or four storied concrete mansions, many turned into home-stay residences. We stay at one such premises. Nearby, an ancient village house is sandwiched among all the new structures. Seafood is served along the beach as the tide rises to near the front street, while fishermen attend to sorting their fishing nets by the beach.

Again as if by karma, a few houses away from our randomly picked home-stay house is the White Dolphin Research and Conservation Center. I get curious and poke my head into this house with sign boards outside. The *couple in charge and living there turn out to be the daughter and son-in-law of renowned wildlife biologist Professor Pan Wenshi of Beijing University. Pan was famous first for his long-term study of the Giant Panda, later for his research on the White-headed Langur of Guangxi, and lastly for Chinese White Dolphin conservation along this bay.*

In 2008, his daughter Pan Yue and son-in-law Zhao Yi closed down their successful business in Beijing in order to commit to the continuation of senior Pan's life-long dedication to wildlife research and conservation. It is with such ideals that they set up home at this coastal delta to protect the endangered White Dolphin of China. Today, from the former small number of maybe 40, the population has grown to over 300. All local fishermen realize the significance of this marine mammal and consider it part of their mission to protect the species.

Pan Yue explains to me that the so-called "pink dolphin" that lives near Hong Kong in waters at the mouth of the Pearl River delta is actually the same species of dolphin as those they work on, the China White Dolphin. However, as the dolphin grows from infant to adult then to old age, its color changes from dark to lighter and gradually takes on a slight pinkish taint when reflected in daylight. Pan Yue's home pet however, is not a dolphin, but a most active border collie in black and white stripes, a constant reminder of her father's most famous subject of research, the Giant Panda.

The panda has been for decades a symbol for China. That panda, however, has grown up, and it now has dagger-like canines. Not a passive vegetarian but a carnivore now, it is no longer a tamed servant of the West, and definitely not a pet.

Pan and Zhao / 潘岳和趙毅

海岸城鎮奇遇記 第一章 廣西篇

現在已經是二〇二二年十二月了，又到了一年的尾聲。巧的是，十年前的十二月，是我首次與一號邊界碑相遇的時間。這個標示著中國陸地邊界開端的界碑是大清王朝於一八九〇年設立的，全線可以從此處蜿蜒延伸逾二萬二千公里。在那次的旅程中，我們深入考察了中國與越南、老撾、緬甸的邊境，最後在雲南西部的邊界畫下休止符，但實際上，我們涉足的僅是中國陸地邊境線的一小部分。

一號界碑同時也是中國漫長海岸線的起點，從這裡開始，可向外延伸一萬八千公里。此番旅途，我們將向東行，沿著中國綿長的海岸線探訪大小漁村、港口，還有離岸不遠的小島飛地。礙於時間所限，我打算以上海作為終點，這樣至少也能走過中國海岸線的三分之一。

廣西省欽州縣是一號界碑的所在地，設立界碑的彼時，它還在廣東省的管轄範圍內。那時的中國正處於群狼環伺的包圍圈中，西方列強津津樂道地瓜分著內陸與沿海城市的治外法權。英國接管許多中國海關，大量收取現金充當中國政府的戰爭賠款。法國則掌控著中國的郵政服務。當時法國已經殖民了越南全境和大部分的老撾，所以它仗著其殖民地版圖之大，不僅獲得了政治、經濟和海事的特權，還擴張了它的宗教滲透影響。一八八三年結束的中法戰爭讓法國嘗盡了甜頭，中國「奉獻」出的多項特權其

中之一，就包括允許法國從沿海地區派遣傳教士進入內陸，甚至可以深入西藏。

位於中越邊境的善德村附近有一座法國天主教堂，最初於一八五〇年在竹山建立，一八八三年戰爭勝利後，法國人對其進行了擴建和鞏固。鄰近村莊的居民都是京族人，又稱作「越族」，這是個中國境內人口不足三萬人的少數民族。但在海灣另一面的越南，京族人口則要多得多，他們佔越南總人口的百分之八十六，約七千五百萬人，主宰著該國的政治與商業。然而在中國這邊，他們主要都是傳統的漁民，過著靠海吃海的樸素生活。

法國人的宗教殖民計畫在中國境內進行的並不算順利，但是小範圍內也有一定程度的影響力。起初，當地只有一位法國神父，也僅僅能夠感化二十八戶家庭共一百三十二人。隨後，教堂擴大了規模，並增加了一所修女院，另外派駐了十名修女。一九五二年共產黨接管中國全境後，大約卅戶人家超過兩百名信徒離開了中國，永久移居越南。之後的很長一段時間裡，教堂活動一直是被禁止的，直到一九八四年，也就是文化大革命結束近十年後才得以恢復。到了九〇年代，當地的天主教徒總數達到了三百六十人。今天，這座教堂可以容納大約兩百人，儘管沒有神父常駐，但當地長者仍會在復活節、聖誕節等特殊宗教節日組織活動，每個星期日也會有人群趕來做彌撒。

金灘，順著其名「金色沙灘」之意，同樣也是京族人的居住地。昔日默默無聞的漁村，如今已變身為旅遊天堂，許多自由行旅客選擇留宿於沙灘邊的民宿酒店，我們也不例外，挑了一家緊鄰金色沙灘的小旅館，選個好位置將房車停好，便可坐觀潮汐變化之美。浪花拍打著岸邊的水泥防波堤，最後湧至我的腳邊。疫情讓這兒的價格划算了不少，陽台海景房此時僅需每晚一百二十元人民幣。

當地的漁船挺有特色，船頭是傾斜的平頭，錨固於岸邊，每日清晨出海撒網。從前都是以竹材或木

French church at San De / 善德村的法國教會

Inside of church / 教堂內部

材造船，現在有了現代材料，當地人會將船隻的下半部改用保麗龍，以增強浮力。在海上，他們能捕獲綠蟹、藍蟹以及各種近岸魚類，而在潮退後廣闊的沙泥灘上，也有著大批種類豐富的貝類。當地有一個詞「趕海」，近幾年在網路上也算個熱詞，意指人們趁著海水退潮時，紛紛步出家門，追隨著退去的海浪，在灘塗上收集各式貝殼和海洋生物，好像白鷺等濱鳥覓食的情景，非常有趣。

在中國境內不足三萬的京族人之中，六十七歲的蘇春發擁有其獨特地位。他被選為中國非物質文化遺產傳承人之一，也是京族特有的單弦樂器國家級藝術家。最近，由他指揮的一個由十六位成員組成的京族單弦樂團正受邀進行全國巡演中，在電視和社交媒體上他們也擁有不小的曝光度。

但蘇先生可不僅僅是藝術家，他是個多才多藝，實打實的全能型戰士。在六〇年代，他曾是一名電子工程師，負責為漁船製作無線電對講機。如今，他是當地村裡消防志願隊的隊長，每當有火災發生時，他都會第一時間駕著他的越野車趕往事故現場。

與蘇先生的相遇真是緣分帶來的巧合，彼時他正望向大海，騎著機車巡邏海岸，可謂是颯爽英姿。蘇先生目前領導著一個專門查緝走私的小組，通常是針對中越之間小型商品的走私，如香煙、中藥材、海鮮和一些雜貨。這類的走私事件並不少見，畢竟從越南到這附近的萬尾島，搭船最多只要十五分鐘。

蘇先生還是個企業家，他有三條漁船，平日會出租給漁民，有時漁獲也能充當租金。他還涉獵批發漁業，顛峰期每天採購的海產能超過一噸，然後統通送往鄰省販賣。但

是因為中國的海洋保育政策，如今每年的五月到九月都是禁漁期，好在禁漁期間每條漁船能得到七千元人民幣政府發的補償。

經歷豐富的蘇先生建議我們參觀一下當地的京族海神廟，這些寺廟是京族人祈求海神，保佑出海平安的聖地。算上越南，全世界僅存十二座此類的廟宇。由此可見，中國的京族人數雖然稀少，但仍是這一民族古老傳統不可或缺的傳承者。

在進入廣東之前，我們又參觀了廣西的另一漁港，同樣位於欽州的三浪灣。這片海灣經過大規模的改造，如今已變成了一處休閒公園。昔日的漁村民居已被三四層的混凝土大樓所取代，許多被改建為民宿，我們就住在其中一家。離我們不遠處，一座古老的村屋被大批嶄新的建築環繞包夾著，有時看著它像一個新世界裡無所適從的老靈魂，有時又覺得新與舊一同構成的畫面也不失和諧。海水漲潮時，沙灘上會有忙碌著賣海鮮的人，漁民們則在一旁認認真真地整理漁網。

彷彿是命中注定，離我們隨意選擇的民宿幾戶之外，就是白海豚研究與保護中心。我當然按捺不住好奇心，立刻就小心地去打探情況，這才發現，住在這裡的負責人夫婦竟是著名野生生物學家，北京大學潘文石教授的女兒潘岳和女婿趙毅。潘教授最初因長期研究大熊貓而聞名，後來他又致力於廣西白頭葉猴的研究，晚年

Coastal hotel / 海岸旅館
Boat out to sea / 出海去

Sunset on horizon / 地平線上的日落
Old house among new / 被新建築包圍的老屋

又來到這片海灣開展中華白海豚的保育項目。

二〇〇八年，潘岳和趙毅放棄了他們在北京的成功事業，全身心投入於潘教授的野生動物保育工作。正是懷著這樣善良的信念，他們在這片沿海三角洲重新建立了自己的小家，來保護中國瀕危白海豚們的大家。在他們的努力下，當地白海豚數量已從原先的僅四十幾頭增長到超過三百頭。也是在他們的呼籲下，當地漁民都逐漸意識到了這種海洋哺乳動物的重要性，並將保護牠們視為自己的使命。

潘岳跟我說，生活在香港附近珠江口海域所謂的「粉紅海豚」其實跟他們研究的是同一物種，都是中華白海豚。只不過隨著海豚從幼年到成年再到老年，其顏色會從深變淺，逐漸變成在陽光照射下呈現的淡粉紅色調。但是潘岳家的寵物可不是海豚，而是隻活潑的黑白條紋花色的邊境牧羊犬，看起來會讓人聯想到他父親最有名的研究對象大熊貓。

幾十年來，憨態可掬大熊貓一直都是中國的象徵。不過，熊貓般溫順的中國也已經長大，現在它擁有比首般的犬齒，不再是被動的素食者，而是有能力主動出擊的肉食者了。如今，相信不僅是西方人，全世界的人們都不會僅僅只把它當成一個逆來順受的「寵物」了。

Fishing at low tide / 在退潮時捕魚

海岸城鎮奇遇記（第二章 廣東篇）

COASTAL ESCAPADE (Part 2 Guangdong)

Guangxi, Guangdong, Fujian, Zhejiang – Dec 2022 to Jan 2023

COASTAL ESCAPADE (Part 2 Guangdong)

Continuing our wandering along China's southern coast, we enter Guangdong from the west and visit several large and small fishing ports: Wu Shi, a small fishing village on the west coast of Lei Zhou Peninsula opposite Hainan Island, Bo He Port at Mao Ming County, Dong Ping Port at Yang Jiang County, and Shan Wei Port east of Hong Kong. The latter three are among the top ten fishing ports of China, all located along the coast of Guangdong.

Visiting so many fishing ports can become quite confusing, as the image of one begins to blur into that of another, each with large or small fleets at anchor inside their bay as typhoon shelter. However, individuals we interview help make each port distinctive, as each gives a personal narrative about their occupation. Buying fresh caught seafood at wholesale bargain prices right at the pier also becomes our daily routine, as each evening we devour the choicest catch at a great discount.

Perhaps the experience of forty-seven year old fishing boat owner Xie Jingzhong of Mao Ming, the huge port of Bo He, is a good representation of the state of affairs these days. His account defines a microcosm of China's coastal fishing industry through a single unit's operations during the last decade. It also offers a comparison to my experience and my former accounts of traveling out to

Buying seafood / 愉快地買海鮮

sea with two fishing trawlers from nearby Hainan Island forty years ago in 1984, just after national policy was liberalized to allow private ownership of boats.

Xie has been into fishing for over thirty years and now owns two trawlers. Of his four sons, three are involved in his fishing business. One prefers to work in Guangzhou, as he considers fisherman's work very hard and also dirty. Xie the father hires 13 workers on his two boats, paying them between 6,000 to 7,000 RMB per month. Each outing to sea takes around a week to ten days. Near Bo He, the fishery is quite rich with fish, shrimp, crab, and a large variety of shellfish.

During the summer, due to hot weather, the catch rots faster, so they must return to port every five to seven days. Winter catch is of lesser varieties, but each trip takes up to ten days. Between November to February, the mantis

Eel catch / 鰻魚
Fish catch into harbor / 漁獲上岸

shrimp are fat and big and each round may yield up to 500 kilos of such shrimp. Smaller ones are sold at 10 to 15 RMB per catty or half kilo. But the clearer big ones can fetch over 20 RMB per catty. It is the most profitable catch during the winter.

Between May and August each year is the fishing ban months and everyone takes a break and relaxes at home. Xie's workers would each receive 2,000 RMB as compensation from the government then. When September comes around, they will come back to work. Xie's original investment into the two trawlers was between six to seven million, and each month he has to repay the loan in amounts of over a hundred thousand RMB. After deducting workers' salaries, fuel costs and maintenance, he can still net a profit of one to two million per year.

Each boat owner can also receive between 50,000 to 200,000 RMB as compensation during fish ban months, depending on the sizes of the boat. Large fishing boats can get as much as half a million to one million in compensation for not being out to sea. That is a hefty sum, all paid for by the government in order to preserve ocean marine life during crucial months for reproduction. So, despite hard work, the return is quite lucrative for some modern-day boat owners.

Fish Vender / 賣魚的攤販

At Bo He port is a huge red banner at the port landing warning fishing boats not to sail into politically sensitive waters, and especially to avoid entering territorial waters of neighbor countries. Such literal warnings would never be noticed by western media with a provocative agenda. While I would not mind declaring my own biases and prejudices arising from being Chinese, I detest other "journalists" who avoid declaring theirs while always maintaining they are perfectly non-biased and neutral, hiding behind branded media while proclaiming it to be "fair" reporting. This is a perfect reversal of my own US training as a journalist.

East of Mao Ming is Yang Jiang County, also by the coast. It is here at Dong Ping Port that I watch and enjoy the last sunset of 2022. Next morning, on January 1, I visit Tai O, an old village that used to be very prosperous. A village by the same name on Lantau Island Hong Kong has seen a few of our new projects during the pandemic. That Tai O fishing village has declined in half a century from over 30,000 people to 3,000, while this Tai O here has perhaps only a couple hundred people remaining. Compare that to its heyday when it had a nicely built chamber of commerce, a fortified bank and streets of merchants. In fact a circulating legend has it that when the Qianlong Emperor secretly visited the area during the epoch of the Qing Dynasty, Tai O was known as Xiao O (meaning small bay). Seeing the prosperity, the Emperor declared that the name should be changed to Tai O, meaning "big bay".

Despite its remoteness today, and the somewhat desolate state of its affairs, the government has recently been pouring in money hoping to turn it into a tourist site with some historical relevance and cultural value.

Yang Jiang, however, offers something else special beyond its big fishing port of Bo He and its small little-known fishing village of Tai O. Along the inside of this huge bay are oyster farmers, in places spreading far into the distance with their framework structures just above the tidal high water, the growing oysters suspended right below. We visit 47 years old Feng Xueyong who is one of the most successful oyster farmers in the area.

Feng came from the countryside and thus speaks an earthy dialect while adding a few qualifying foul verbs, adverbs, or adjectives to accentuate each sentence. "I have lost two to three f#$%ing millions investing in growing Ju Xia like my neighbors here," he lamented. He is speaking about his failure at farming bamboo prawns. Pointing to the huge covered ponds as we drive along narrow dike roads surrounded by ponds on both sides. Now he has figured out what is the best way to make a profit - through oyster farming.

"It was 1991 and I was fifteen when I went to Zhanjiang to look for work," says Feng. "In the beginning, I worked with a shrimp farm, and two years later thought I had learned the trade and started my own business back home," Feng continues. "That first venture failed badly. Later I had a chance to work in oyster farming, observing and learning the process." He opened his own oyster farm, now with 400 acres and 500 oyster grids

Chamber of Commerce / 大澳商會舊址
Tai O hostel / 大澳客棧

and yielding 100,000 catty live oysters in a year. They are shipped to Shenzhen, Zhuhai and Hong Kong.

While we are interviewing him, a call comes in ordering a ton of oysters. Each year, his revenue averages between seven and eight million RMB. After deducting costs of two to three million, he still can have a very lucrative profit. Costs include hiring four workers, each working from 7am to 5pm during the busy season from September to December. Each worker makes 6500 to 7,000 RMB per month, amounting to half a million each year. The land he rents costs him 100,000 per year.

As his pond has a water gate for intake and drainage during high and low tide, twice a month his team need to drain and refill the seawater, and that requires two to three days to complete. This provides fresh nutrients for the growing oysters, which are suspended on strings under the bamboo grids. Currently, there are only two oyster farmers in the village of Sanya where he is. Others are all into prawn farming.

Now it has been 31 years since Feng had his own business and became successful enough to own the largest hotel and restaurant in the nearby town of Dagou. His wife manages all that. His son is in second year of university in Guangzhou and his daughter in third year high school studying art. Each year, that alone costs 200,000 RMB, including the cost of a special tutor so that she may eventually enter an art institute. He keeps a home in Guangzhou where the children live, and felt that neither kid would want to succeed his business, as it is very hard work, though profitable.

After Yangjiang, I make a cursory stop at Shanwei, another large fishing port east of Hong Kong. By now, looking at boats returning to port and unloading their catch has become more or less redundant. And I have been feasting on various kinds of fresh seafood for over a week, and am worried that I may start smelling like one. We turn inland to make a bee line toward Fujian, the next province.

In between, I make a stop at Mei Zhou to revisit the round houses of the Hakka people that I had first visited twenty years ago. The area, once one of the poorest regions of Guangdong, has made major progress. We stay at a very nice boutique hotel converted from an old schoolhouse. Because of its age, it seems haunted, especially because nearby are a number of abandoned old fortress-like houses, built in that distinctive round shape largely as defense against bandits in more turbulent times. Stories from decades ago note that US satellite photos revealed these structures and the US spooks speculated that they must be ballistic missile silos.

l turned into hotel / 舊校舍改裝的旅館   Dilapidated house / 破舊的房屋   Slogan from the past / 來自過去的標語

While taking a peek into ruins of one of these houses, we run into a Ms. Yao fetching water from a hand-pumped well to water her plantation of vegetables in the interior courtyard. According to her, the house has a history of over a hundred years. The courtyard well is over forty years old, but the water is still good.

There used to be fifteen households within the same clan living together inside the half-circular house. They were composed of three senior members of the clan and their descendants. As the clan grew, the house was expected to grow gradually until someday it would close the gap to form a circular house. But that would never happen in this case, as such tradition and heritage have been discontinued among today's families. Even close relatives would prefer to each build their own more modern multi-story houses. Such buildings, each named lou meaning "mansion", are mushrooming up throughout all the Hakka region of Mei Zhou.

Today there is only one old man, an uncle of Ms. Yao, still living in a dilapidated and shabby unit, raising chicken and ducks. At one point, eleven of the families decided to jointly restore the old house as a home-stay specimen to attract tourists. But the remaining four families did not agree, and the house remains in ruins today. I somehow like this half-finished circular house for its dynamics, as often I find perfection rather boring. Unfortunately, the momentum of tradition is long dead in a fast-track society embracing modernity.

Hakka fortress house / 客家堡壘式房屋
Circular house on ground / 從地面上看到的圓形土樓

海岸城鎮奇遇記 第二章 廣東篇

沿著中國南部海岸線繼續漫遊，從西面進入廣東，我們又不期而遇了幾個大大小小的漁港。位於海南島對面，雷州半島西岸的烏石小漁村，茂名縣的博賀港，陽江縣的東平港，以及香港東邊的汕尾港都留下了獨屬於我們的回憶。後三者都在廣東省的海岸線上，均位列於中國十大漁港。

這麼多漁港參訪下來，實在讓人眼花撩亂，一個個漁港的影像開始模糊交錯。只記得每一處都有或大或小的船隊停泊在避風港裡，安靜的片刻像是一個個漂泊在外的孩子回到了母親溫暖的懷抱。雖然看起來漁港都大同小異，但人的主體性總會讓每個地方都變得特別。我們訪談過的人們都很樂於分享他們的故事、事業，每一個都那麼獨特，讓屬於他們港口都有了獨特的風貌。而我們每日的例行公事，就是在碼頭上以批發價搶購新鮮捕獲的海鮮，然後在晚餐時分大快朵頤，聽著那些平凡又有趣的當地故事，享受以超值折扣價入手的至尊海味。

茂名縣博賀港四十七歲的漁船老闆謝景忠的經歷，能夠生動地反映當下漁業的真實狀況。他透過細緻描述自己的小產業在過去十年間的運營經歷，勾勒出了中國沿海整體漁業的一個生動縮影。同時，這也和四十年前，也就是一九八四年國家政策剛放寬，允許私人擁有船隻後，我與海南島附近的兩艘拖網漁船出海的經歷形成了鮮明對比。

謝先生從事漁業已經超過三十年，如今他擁有兩艘拖網漁船。在他的四個兒子中，有三個參與了他的漁業生意。還有一個選擇在廣州工作，因為他認為漁民的工作太過辛苦，且環境也不衛生。謝先生在兩艘船上雇了十三名工人，每人月薪在六千到七千人民幣之間，每一趟出海大約需要七到十天。在博賀附近，海域的漁獲相當豐富，有魚、蝦、蟹和各式各樣的貝類。

夏季由於天氣炎熱，漁獲容易腐爛，因此他們必須每五至七天就返回港口一次。冬季的漁獲種類較少，所以每一次出海可達十天之久。每年十一月到二月間，蝦蛄碩大肥美，每回合可能捕獲多達五百公斤。小一點的每斤可以賣到十到十五人民幣。那些外型更大、更透亮的蝦蛄，每斤就能賣到二十人民幣以上，這是冬季最賺錢的漁獲。

每年禁漁期，大家都會在家放鬆休息。謝先生的工人們在此期間每人能從政府那裡得到兩千人民幣的補償。九月回來後，他們又會重新上工。謝先生最初投資在這兩艘船上的資金是六到七百萬左右，每個月他得償還超過十萬的貸款。扣除工人薪水、燃油成本和維護費用後，他每年仍能淨賺一到兩百萬。

每位船主在禁漁期間也能根據船隻大小，得到五萬到二十萬人民幣的補償。大型漁船甚至能得到高達五十萬到一百萬的補償。這

Bo He Port fish harvest / 博賀港的漁獲

Red banner warning / 紅色警告橫幅

是一筆可觀的金額，全由政府支付，目的在於保護海洋生命，在繁殖的關鍵月分避免過度捕撈。所以儘管工作辛苦，但對於一些現代船主來說，回報可謂是相當豐厚的。

在博賀港頭，一幅醒目的巨大紅橫幅猶如警告的長笛，提醒著每一艘漁船不要觸碰政治敏感的水域，尤其是要避免進入鄰國的領海。這種直白的警告，卻經常被帶有挑釁意圖的西方媒體視而不見。我完全不介意坦承自己作為華人看待問題會帶有一定的主觀性偏見，但是我對那些避而不談自身的偏見，卻總自詡完全公正無私，躲在知名媒體品牌後面，大張旗鼓宣揚「公正、中立」報導的「新聞工作者」深惡痛絕。這完全違背了我在美國接受的記者訓練。

越過茂名向東，是同樣臨海的陽江縣。正是在這裡的東平港，我欣賞到了二〇二二年的最後一次日落。翌日一月一日，我拜訪了大澳，這個曾經繁華一時的老村莊。大澳於我們而言可是個熟悉的名字，在疫情期間，我們在香港大嶼山上同名的大澳村開展了數個新項目。那個大澳漁村在半個世紀的時間裡，人口從三萬多降至只剩三千，而這裡的大澳，如今大概只剩下幾百人。回想它的全盛時期，也曾有過氣派的商會、戒備森嚴但絡繹不絕的銀行和熙熙攘攘的商販街道。傳說乾隆皇帝曾微服私訪這片地區，在清朝時期這裡被稱為小澳，意為小海灣。而正是親眼見證了當地

的繁榮，所以皇帝欽定將其改名為大澳，從名字上就體現了它的盛極一時。

儘管今日的大澳偏僻且有些荒涼，政府卻不打算完全放棄它，最近還追加了投資，希望將其打造成具有歷史意義和文化價值的旅遊景點。

除了擁有壯闊的大漁港博賀和人所鮮知的小漁村大澳，陽江市還有很多其他的獨特之處。在這巨大海灣的內側，牡蠣養殖戶密布，點綴於遼闊水域。他們的架構僅高於滿潮線，牡蠣吊掛其下，隨波逐流。

我們探訪了四十七歲的馮學庸，他是當地最成功的牡蠣養殖大戶，嘴裏講著土話方言，時不時還夾雜著幾句髒話，是個十分鮮活的人物。「我跟這的不少鄰居一樣，投資養竹蝦賠了他媽的兩三百萬。」說的是失敗的經驗，但我從他臉上看不到太強烈的懊悔，也許是因為，正是之前的經歷才給他帶來了現在的成功。我們開車經過狹窄的道路，兩側盡是池塘。他望著池塘的臉上盡是滿足，因

Tai O village / 大澳村   Overview of Tai O / 俯瞰大澳灣

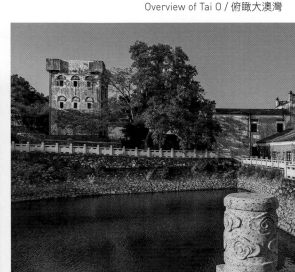

Oyster farm over water / 水面上的牡蠣養殖架
Harvesting oyster / 採收牡蠣

為他已經摸索出了最賺錢的門道：牡蠣養殖。

馮先生回憶說：「那時候是一九九一年，我十五歲就去湛江找工作，在一家蝦場打工。兩年之後，我以為已經學到不少，就信心滿滿地回家創業了。」他繼續說道：「第一次創業賠慘了。後來無意間接觸了牡蠣養殖，覺得這也是個好產業，就花了不少時間精力摸透了整個過程。」皇天不負有心人，他最終開設了自己的牡蠣場，現在擁有四百畝土地和五百個養殖架，年產活牡蠣達十萬斤，產品遠銷深圳、珠海和香港。

我們採訪他的間隙，一通訂購一噸牡蠣的電話打進來。這可是筆大單，我們於是談到他收入情況，得知他的年收入平均在七八百萬人民幣之間。扣除兩三百萬的成本，這個利潤也是相當可觀。成本包括四名工人，每人在九月至十二月的旺季從早上七點工作到下午五點，每人月薪六千五百至七千元人民幣。算下來，相當於工人薪資成本一年近五十萬，土地租賃上一年是大概花費十萬。

他的池塘設有水閘，可以在潮漲潮退時進行排放和灌溉，每兩週進行一次，每次需要兩到三天完成這個過程。這樣做能為吊掛在竹架子底下成長中的牡蠣提供新鮮營養。目前，他所在的三亞村算上他只有兩位牡蠣養殖戶，其他人都投身於蝦養殖業。

Circular house from air / 鳥瞰圓形土樓

三十一個寒暑匆匆過去，馮先生走過初創期的艱辛，捱過途中的種種壓力，最終打造了自己的「商業帝國」，成功到擁有了鄰近小鎮上最大的酒店和餐廳，可謂是風光無限。目前這兩項生意都是他的妻子在全權打理。他們的兒子正在廣州讀大學二年級，女兒在讀高中三年級，主修藝術。每年僅孩子們的教育開支就要二十萬人民幣，他們還為女兒請了家教，以期她能考進頂尖的藝術學院。他在廣州還有一處房產，孩子們就住在那裡。不過他覺得兩個孩子都不會想接手他的生意，因為這工作雖然好賺，但也實在太辛苦了。

離開陽江後，我順道在汕尾稍作停留，這是香港東邊的另一個大型漁港。如今，觀察船隻歸港卸貨的景象對我來說已經變得有點多餘。過去一週我們已經吃了太多海鮮了，我都擔心自己快要變成海鮮，走到哪裡都散發著魚腥味了。於是我們轉向內陸，直奔福建省。

途中，我再次造訪了梅州，那裡有我睽違了二十年的客家圓形土樓。這片廣東最貧窮的地區，現在已取得了翻天覆地的進步。我們住在一家由舊校舍改建的旅店。由於它的古老，這地方彷彿帶著些幽靈的氣息，尤其是因為附近有許多廢棄的、堡壘般的圓形房屋，它們大多是動盪時期為了抵禦盜匪而建。有趣的是，數十年前，美國的衛星捕捉到了這些建築，當時美國情報部門還臆測它們可能是導彈發射井。

窺探其中一座土樓遺跡時，我們遇到了一位姓姚的女士，她正在用手抽水井給內院的菜園澆水。她說，這房子有一百多年的歷史了，院子裡的井也有四十年了，但水質依舊良好。

這座半圓形的房子曾經住著十五戶同宗族的家庭，由三位宗族的長老及其後代組成。隨著宗族的擴大，大家都期望房子也能被逐漸擴建，直至有朝一日合攏成一個完整的圓形。但現在看來，這個「圓」或許永遠也不能圓滿了，因為現代家庭已經不再延續這種傳統的居住模式了。即便是血脈相連的親人，也各自青睞於築造更為現代、層層疊疊的獨立屋新居。那樣的建築，在客家的梅州大地上如雨後春筍般冒出，每幢皆冠以「樓」之名，意味著「豪宅」。

土樓僅存的居民是姚女士的伯父，一位老翁，在簡陋老舊的一隅，養著雞鴨，孤獨地守著舊時光。曾有一刻，十一戶族人決意攜手，將這古宅煥然一新，打造成民宿，吸引遊客駐足。然而，剩餘四家卻意見不一，以致於這宅院至今仍舊荒廢。對這座未圓之圓屋，我卻怪喜歡它不完整的生命力，因為在我眼裡，盡善盡美往往透著乏味。可惜，在這個快軌社會，傳統的韻律早已在現代化的懷抱中黯然逝去。

Old traditional house / 梅州老屋

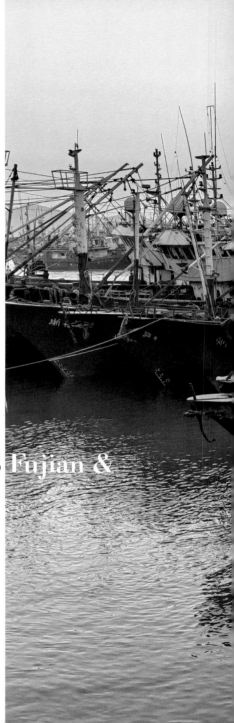

（第三章　福建與浙江篇）

海岸城鎮奇遇記

COASTAL ESCAPADE (Part 3 Fujian & Zhejiang)

Guangxi, Guangdong, Fujian, Zhejiang – Dec 2022 to Jan 2023

COASTAL ESCAPADE *(Part 3 Fujian & Zhejiang)*

From the southern border of Fujian Province to the city of Xiamen is an easy drive of 260 km and three hours by car. There is a tourist village with boutique hotels by the bay where the narrow alley streets are filled with restaurants and small shops. One such shop is a photo studio recreating a set from the Cultural Revolution with backdrops, costumes, etc. It seems quite popular with tourists, even for kids. There are also plenty of snack eateries, many of which sell small oysters cooked in the shell. These go for a meager 10 RMB for 15 pieces, compared to fine oysters in Hong Kong fetching 30 RMB a piece - a difference in price of 30 folds. Such small pieces are harvested after only six months, whereas the larger pieces in Yang Jiang and Hong Kong take three years or more to mature.

We sail for fifteen minutes across the bay to spend a half-day at Gulangyu, an island enclave with plenty of colonial architecture. It was once a concession area for Western powers that had carved up China's coastal cities for commercial and trade interests. The old church stands out amongst other well-preserved buildings. Many are now turned into cafes, shops and hotels for tourists.

Leaving Xiamen driving northeast along the coast for another hour, we end up at Quanzhou. This is an ancient city, once the center for much maritime trade. I have yearned to visit Quanzhou since the early 1980s when for one year I focused on exploring China's Islamic heritage. Quanzhou has one of the earliest mosques in China, opened in 1009 during the Northern Song Dynasty over a thousand years ago, when Arab and Persian merchants arrived by sea. As such, it has been included in China's first-class list of national protected heritage sites since 1961. We find a hotel, the Overseas Chinese Hotel, within walking distance to the Qing Jing Mosque, meaning "clear and clean" mosque.

After lunch, we quickly walk over to the mosque, only to find the gate locked. A sign outside states that, due to the pandemic, the place is closed to religious service as well as to visitors. As a guard is sitting inside the gate, I wave for him to come over. He steps forward apprehensively and shakes his head and hands, then says that most people living inside have tested positive for the Covid virus and he cannot open the gate. I raise my voice and ask him to call for the Ahung, a generic title for the head of a Muslim community. He seems to ponder this and leaves momentarily.

Shortly after, a man with a little white cap and mask comes up to the gate. I already have a copy of my book Islamic Frontiers of China ready in my hand. I put the book up against the gate and tell the gentleman that I have come a long way to deliver this book as a gift to the mosque. My book begins with "seek knowledge, even if you have to go to China," attributed as a quote of the Prophet Mohammed. So, I am following it literally, right at

Eateries of Xiamen / 廈門街頭的小吃攤
Tourist photo studio / 遊客攝影館

this moment.

The gentleman quickly raises his eyes and looks intently as I turn the pages. Soon the gate is open and in flows my small entourage. I am quickly led through the grounds of the mosque with some old walls and pillars, all the while being told stories and legends of old. Afterwards, he leads us to a reception room where tea is being served. Ibrah, short for Ibrahim, now with mask off, turns out to be the head Ahung (similar to an Imam) of the mosque.

Ibrah is originally from Xining in China's northwest province of Qinghai where there is a much larger congregation of Muslims. Tsomo, our Tibetan staff scholar is from that region, too, and soon the two are into full conversation. I also show pictures of two of the mosques in Xining within my book to close the gap of distance.

Ibrah, now 57, came to Quanzhou in 2003 to open a noodle restaurant. He became friends with many local Muslims over the years when he attended services at the mosque. When the senior Ahung resigned in 2010, because Ibrah had been quite fluent since childhood in Arabic and all religious protocol of Islam, he was elected as the new "amateur" Ahung, transitioning from a small businessman to becoming head of the mosque.

Ibrah told us some current background regarding the Muslim community in China. Back home in Xining, every mosque has a school for kids, teaching Islam through the Koran. There are over twenty million Muslims in China today and Arabic is becoming quite popular within these

Ibrah with HM at gate / 易卜拉欣與 HM 隔門交談
Ibrah in old Mosque / 舊清真寺裡的易卜拉欣

communities. Ibrah points out that Henan Province has even more Muslims than the entire Ningxia Hui Autonomous Region. Quanzhou Muslim population is relatively small compared to Ibrah's hometown in Xining where, on any regular day, thousands attend the Great Mosque at the center of the city. On Friday, the congregation may reach over ten thousand. That, I can attest, was true even during my visit in 1984.

Due to China's recent foreign and trade policies with many Middle Eastern countries, Islam concurrently has gained attention and public status, which promotes the learning and use of Arabic a great deal. Ibrah happily told us that he was finally able to go on pilgrimage to Mecca in 2016. Before we took leave, Ibrah gave me a Koran and took us to an adjacent courtyard to look at the new mosque being used today. It was donated and built as a gift in 2009 by the King of Omen when he visited the old mosque.

I leave Quanzhou with an old wish met and travel up the coast to Fuzhou, another city of Fujian. In the town of Mabei ("horse nose"), Yujing ("jade well") fishing village is by a bay with a long

Chen and mud scooters / 陳先生與泥滑板

Oyster shells / 堆積的蠔殼　　Mud scooter parking / 泥滑板「泊車區

mudflat revealed when the tide goes out. Here the locals have maintained traditional use of the mud-scooter, with over a thousand years of history. These ingenuous contraptions are like long, wide skate boards with a handle for the locals to push and glide over the mud with one leg bent. They use them to travel around the mudflats gathering mudskippers or other crustaceans during low tide. Around the Pearl River Delta, including in Hong Kong, similar scooters are used for oyster farming, but these traditions are fast dying out.

Chen Chenggui, 87 years old, is a provincial representative of the Intangible Cultural Heritage holders. Trained since an early age as a carpenter, he began his professional work in the construction of large wooden houses. Later on, he began making mud scooters for his village. Before, each month he might make thirty to forty scooters for between 700 to 800 households of fishermen at Ma Bei. At that time, almost every family would have at least one mud scooter.

Today, only those aged fifty and above use such devices to go out to sea as the tide goes out, called "chasing the ocean". Younger generations have left for work in the cities and often never return, and use of this device is being eclipsed. These days, Chen and his 48-years-old son Kelin only make three to four mud scooters in an entire year.

Twenty years ago, a scooter would cost only 50 RMB, but today it ranges from 300 to 600 depending on size and type of wood being used. A well-made scooter can carry its driver with up to 25 kilos of marine harvest, be it seaweed, green crab, shrimp, fish, octopus, clams or mud skippers.

Recently, there has been a small revival in the use of mud scooters for recreational purpose. Since the father and son were featured on Central Television, last year a tour outfitter in Fuzhou ordered 40 scooters from Kelin. CERS

Long bridge to Zhou Shan / 通往舟山的跨海大橋

intends to turn this age-old yet functional device into the basis of a modern experiential and educational sport, first in Hong Kong, and later wherever there are expanse of tidal mud flats. Before departing, we negotiate purchase of a well-used mud scooter and tie it on our roof rack to bring home as a specimen.

Xiapu is some two hours away, near the northernmost end of Fujian Province. While the bay here is boasted to be the largest mudflat in China, my attention turns instead to a small fishing port. Lin Jei is owner of the four-story homestay we choose. It stands high above a bay with a small enclave for fishing boats in Dongbi Village of Sansa Township. From boats with sails in the past to motorized fishing boats today, most fishermen have turned to growing seaweed and oyster farming. As far as our eyes can see there is an extensive and expansive labyrinth just above the ocean. These are their grounds for culturing marine products.

Besides the well-adorned modern hostel with five rooms, Lin Jei owns two fishing boats with ten workers on them. Each worker is paid around 11,000 RMB per month, and each boat produces a revenue of 150,000 to 200,000 RMB per month. In the summer, each round of fishing at sea takes two to three days, whereas winter rounds would be a week to ten days. These are mainly for shrimp and mantis shrimp net fishing. Between

Sunset at Dongbi / 東壁的日落

May and August, no fishing is allowed, giving the marine life a chance to recover.

Seaweed and oyster farming are newly introduced only within the last couple years but have become popular very quickly. Fresh seaweed can be sold for two to three RMB a catty, whereas the dried item goes for sixty to seventy depending on grades. Oysters are harvested over six months cycles. We see many groups of local women working on stuffing young oysters into nets, to be lifted in huge bundles by cranes and dropped onto a boat, moored on the side and taken out to sea for culturing.

Our next and final stop is at Zhoushan of Zhejiang Province. This is one of the ten largest fishing ports along China's coast, across the bay from Ningpo where many prominent shipping families come from. It is also within sight of the Yangtze delta and Shanghai, connected by a long sea bridge spanning almost fifty kilometers.

By now we have been overwhelmed with images and numbers related to fisheries and make only a cursory visit to the port and interview some owners and deck hands of one fishing boat returning from sea. The manager of the boat came from northeastern China to settle here. His boat has five workers. Three are deck hands dealing with fishing; a captain and the owner make six in total.

They work through the night and return to port in the morning. Each trip may yield up to 20,000 catties, or 10,000 kilos of fish. At times, catching 5,000 to 7,000 catties would be considered a low yield. Currently, between November to February, the largest catch is mantis shrimp, just as we see; basket upon basket is being unloaded onto small tractors to be hauled inside the processing depot *adjacent to the mooring.*

Winter is crab season and they can catch up to 1,000 kilos each trip. The ones with roe are the best during this time, and a good one may fetch up to 250 RMB. As their boat is small, they return from sea to port daily once they fill their hold. One such trip may yield a return of 200,000 RMB or higher.

Some of the numbers I reported along my journey may seem mundane and boring, but it may serve as a baseline for future comparative study regarding this subject of period in time. We made a final stop at nearby Dong Po To, one of the four most important Buddhist sacred sites in China. Here, we offer thanks to a safe and successful journey.

Thus ends our rather fast-track, month-long excursion along China's southern and eastern seacoast. The constant diet of seafood has been interesting, as have been the homestays and boutique guesthouses. As we drive into Shanghai, we look forward to taking a long-awaited reprieve in one of the privately owned villas in the Shanghai Aman, courtesy of one of our CERS directors. Smelling like fish ourselves, we won't be ordering seafood for dinner!

Sacred Buddhist site / 佛教聖地東普陀
Temple at Dong Po To / 東普陀的寺廟

海岸城鎮奇遇記　第三章 福建與浙江篇

從福建南部的省界到廈門開車只有二百六十公里，用時三小時，這跟我們以往大多數的路程比起來算是相當輕鬆。海灣旁有一個旅遊度假村，村裡有著形形色色的小旅館，狹窄的巷弄內，餐廳和小商店林立。其中一家店鋪是一間攝影工作室，似乎很受遊客、甚至是孩童的歡迎，它重現了文化大革命時期的場景，提供背景板、服裝等道具。村子裡還有許多小吃店，多半販售帶殼現烤的小牡蠣。這些小牡蠣十五顆僅售十元人民幣，相較於香港的精品牡蠣每顆三十元人民幣的售價，差價竟高達三十倍。這些小牡蠣只需養殖六個月即可收穫，而陽江和香港的大牡蠣則需要至少三年才能成熟。

僅需十五分鐘船程，就能從廈門穿越海灣到達鼓浪嶼，我們在那裡度過了半天時光。鼓浪嶼是一個擁有豐富殖民地建築風格的小島，它曾是西方列強為方便瓜分中國沿海城市而設的自由商業貿易區，也就是租界。一座古老的教堂在一眾保存完好的建築物中顯得尤為突出。許多建築現在已被用作咖啡館、商店和酒店。

離開廈門，沿著海岸向東北方再駕車一個小時，我們來到了泉州。這是一座古老的城市，曾是眾多海上貿易的中心。早在八〇年代初，在我全身心投入於中國伊斯蘭教歷史和遺產的那一整年時間裡，我就多次渴望訪問泉州。因為泉州擁有中國最早的清真寺之一，於一千多年前的北宋時期，西元一〇〇九年開設，當時還有阿拉伯和波斯商

Western House of Gulangyu / 鼓浪嶼的西式建築　　　　Gulangyu Western church / 鼓浪嶼的西方教堂

人經海路絡繹前來。因此，自一九六一年以來，它就被納入中國一級國家保護遺址名錄。我們找了一家在清淨寺步行距離內的酒店，名字叫華僑大酒店，清淨寺的清淨二字意味著清潔和純淨，無慾又無求。

午餐後，我們快步走向清真寺，卻發現大門緊鎖。門外的告示牌上顯示，由於疫情，此地暫停宗教活動也暫時不對遊客開放。我不想放棄，看到門裡有個警衛坐著，我便向他招手示意，他看到後走了過來，但是又在安全距離內停了下來，搖搖頭擺擺手，說裡面的大多數人確診了新冠肺炎，他不能開門。我加大了大嗓門，請求他去叫他們的阿訇，阿訇是一個穆斯林社區領袖的通稱。他似乎在考慮這個請求，隨即離開了一會兒。

不久之後，一位戴著小白帽和口罩的先生走到大門前，此時我手中已經準備好了我的成書《中國邊疆的伊斯蘭》。我將書貼在門上，告訴這位先生，我特地遠道而來，想將這本書作為禮物獻給清真

Front of Mosque / 清真寺正面

寺。我的書開篇引用了先知穆罕默德的話：「尋求知識，即使必須遠到中國去。」無獨有偶，我此刻正算是身體力行了。

那位先生迅速抬起眼睛，專注地盯著我翻頁。不久，大門打開，我的小隊伍跟我一起被放行。我們被迅速帶領著穿過清真寺的院子，一路上聽著從前的故事和傳說，四周是一些古老的牆壁和柱子。之後，他帶我們一行人進入一個已經擺好茶水的接待室，屋內並無他人。此時，這位易卜拉欣先生才終於摘下了口罩，原來他就是這座清真寺的阿訇（類似於伊瑪目）。

易卜拉欣原籍中國西北部青海省的西寧，那裡的穆斯林群體規模更大。我們的藏族同事措姆也來自那裡，不久，他們兩人便投入了熱切的交談。我向他展示了我書中兩座西寧清真寺的照片，以此拉近彼此的距離。

五十七歲的易卜拉欣於二〇〇三年來到泉州開了一家麵館。多年來，他透過參加當地清真寺的活動結交了許多本地的穆斯林朋友。二〇一〇年，當上一任資深的阿訇辭職時，易卜拉欣憑藉著從小便能流利地使用阿拉伯語，且熟知伊斯蘭所有宗教禮儀，被推選為新一代的「業餘」阿訇，從一個小商人轉變為一座清真寺的領袖。

易卜拉欣向我們介紹了一些關於中國穆斯林社群的現狀。在他的家鄉西寧，每座清真寺都有附屬學校，並透過古蘭經教授伊斯蘭教義。今天，中國有超過二千萬的穆斯林，河南省的穆斯林人數甚至超過了整個寧夏回族自治區的穆斯林人數，而阿拉伯語在這些社群中的普及度相當高。與易卜拉欣的家鄉西寧相比，泉州的穆斯林人口相對較少，在西寧，任何一個平凡的一天，都有數千人會參加市中心大清真寺的禮拜。到了星期五，參拜的人數甚至可能超過一萬。這一點我可以作證，印象中一九八四年我到訪西寧時，那裡便是易卜拉欣描述中的盛況了。

最近，由於中國對許多中東國家的外交和貿易政策改變，伊斯蘭教開始重新在國際社會上獲得關注和地位，這極大地推廣了阿拉伯語的學習和使用。易卜拉欣高興地告訴我們，二〇一六年的時候他總算是有機會去麥加朝聖一次了。在我們告別之前，他送了我一本古蘭經，並帶我們到相鄰的新清真寺觀看了禮拜。這座新清真寺是二〇〇九年阿曼國王訪問舊清真寺時捐資建給當地的一份禮物。

我得償所願，心滿意足地離開泉州，沿著海岸線北上，前往福建的另一座城市，福州。在馬鼻鎮，

Relics of old mosque / 舊清真寺遺跡

Ibrah from Xining / 來自西寧的易卜拉欣

New mosque / 新清真寺

玉井漁村就坐落於一片潮退時才會顯出面貌的長長泥灘旁。在這裡，當地人還保留著一項擁有超過千年歷史的勞作方式——使用泥滑板。泥滑板這種巧妙的裝置就像是帶把手的，又長又寬的滑板，使用者可以一腿彎曲，一腿借後蹬地的力推著它滑過泥地。他們利用這些泥滑板在退潮時的泥灘上穿梭，捕捉彈塗魚和甲殼類動物。在珠江三角洲周邊，包括香港在內，類似的泥滑板也被用於養蠔，但這些傳統正迅速消逝。

八十七歲的陳長貴是非物質文化遺產持有者的省級代表。他自幼受訓成為木匠，工作後開始建造大型木屋。後來，他開始為村民製作泥滑板。從前的歲月裡，他每個月能為馬鼻鎮的七百到八百戶漁民製作三十到四十個滑板。那時候，幾乎每個家庭都至少擁有一個泥滑板。

反觀現在，只有五十歲以上的老一輩會在退潮出海，趕海時使用這種裝置了。年輕一代已經外出到城市工作，往往再也不會回來，所以泥滑板也漸漸地派不上用場。近些年，陳長貴和他四十八歲的兒子克林一整年只會製作三到四個泥滑板了。

二十年前，一個滑板只需五十元人民幣，但如今，根據尺寸和使用的木材類型，其價格範圍變為從三百到六百元不等。一個作工精良的滑板能夠承載其使用者和多達二十五公斤的漁獲，管你是海藻、綠蟹、蝦、魚、章魚、蛤蜊或彈塗魚，統統裝得住。

近來，泥滑板作為休閒用途有了小幅復興之態。自從父子倆去年在中央電視台亮相後，福州的一家旅行社一下子向克林訂購了四十個泥滑板。中國探險學會打算將這種古老而實用的裝置應用於現代的體驗式教育運動，先在香港推廣，之後可以推廣至任何有

Preparing oyster for planting / 準備養殖的蠔

潮汐泥灘的地方。於是在離開之前，我們與陳氏父子協商，好價購買了一個一看就是飽經風霜的泥滑板，並將它綁在我們車頂的行李架上，作為樣品帶回家。

霞浦縣距離此地約兩小時車程，位於福建省最北端附近。儘管這裡的海灣很出名，擁有傳說中國內最大的泥灘，我的注意力卻還是轉向了一個小漁港。林傑是我們的民宿老闆，他的四層樓小別墅位於三沙鎮東壁村的高處，俯瞰著停泊小漁船們的小島。時間帶來的變化適用於世間萬物。過去的帆船飄過海峽，變成如今的機動漁船，而昔日的漁民們也開始轉做海藻栽培和蠔類養殖。在我們所能看到的範圍內，藍色的大海之上到處是廣闊而繁複的迷宮，這其實是漁民們培育海產品的基地。

除了擁有裝修精美，有五間房間的現代化旅館外，林杰還有兩艘漁船，船上各有十名工人。

Oyster & seaweed farming / 海藻和蠔的養殖基地

每名工人的月薪約為一萬一千元人民幣，每艘船每月的收入為十五萬至二十萬元人民幣。在夏季，每次出海捕魚的時間是兩至三天，而冬季則需一週到十天。這些船主要用於捕撈蝦子與蝦蛄。每年的五月到八月是規定的禁漁期，目的是為了給海洋生物一定的恢復期。

海藻與牡蠣養殖技術僅在過去幾年才被引進，卻快速地普及了起來。新鮮海藻每斤可賣二至三元人民幣，而乾燥海藻根據品質，每斤售價可達六十至七十元人民幣。牡蠣的收穫週期是六個月。我們看見許多當地婦女正在忙於將幼小的牡蠣塞入網袋中，然後由起重機將巨大的捆束吊起，放到停靠在旁的船上，帶出海進行養殖。

我們的下一站也是最後一站，是位於浙江省的舟山。這是中國沿海十大漁港之一，與誕生了許多傳奇航運家族的寧波隔海相望。這裡離長江三角洲和上海也都不遠，有座近五十公里長的跨海大橋將不同的城市互相連結。

行到此處，我們已被漁業相關的資料與數據淹沒，所以在此處僅對港口進行了粗略的參觀，並對一艘剛返港的漁船進行了採訪。出身於中國東北的船老闆有五名工人，三名是負責捕魚的甲板工，加上船長和船主，總共有六人與我們進行了交談。

通常，他們徹夜工作，清晨才返回港口。每趟可能帶回高達兩萬斤，也就是一萬公斤的魚。所以有時捕獲五千到七千斤可能會被視為歉收。目前，在十一月至二月間，最大的收穫是螳螂蝦，也有稱擺尿蝦或蝦蛄。談及此，一籮筐一籮筐的螳螂蝦正好被卸載到小拖車上，然後馬不停蹄地被運送到碼頭旁的加工站內。

冬季是捕蟹季，據了解，漁民每趟可以捕到多達一千公斤的蟹。這個時節帶有蟹卵的算是極品，一隻極品能賣到二百五十元人民幣。由於他們的船較小，一旦貨艙滿載，他們就會從海上返回港口。這樣一趟，可能帶來二十萬元人民幣以上的回報。

你可能覺得我在旅途中記錄的一些數據平平無奇且乏味，但請不要忽視，這些數據很可能在未來某天能作為人們對此主題進行比較研究的基準。我們最後停在中國四大佛教聖地之一的東普陀。我們在此敬佛，為此次安全圓滿的旅程表示感謝。

就這樣，我們結束了在中國南部和東部海岸為期一個月的快速考察之旅。這一路沒斷過的海鮮美食很讓人回味，同樣有趣的還有各色民宿和小旅館帶來的別樣入住體驗。當我們駛入上海時，大家滿心都是終於能在上海養雲安縵的私人渡假村裡好好休息一陣了，當然，這還是托一位我們中國探險學會的董事的福！鑒於我們身上都是海腥味，今天晚餐就破例放棄我最愛的海鮮吧！

Morning rush at Zhou Shan / 舟山繁忙的早晨

緣起星雲

VENERABLE MONK HSING YUN

February 22, 2023

February 22, 2023

VENERABLE MONK HSING YUN
Some private reminisces

The honorable monk Hsing Yun passed away on February 5 at the senior age of 97 in Taiwan. While hundreds of thousands of followers mourn his passing, I would like to recall some of the more private moments I was able to spend with this simple-living monk.

Revered throughout Chinese communities globally, he established over two hundred religious centers in the world during his lifetime. Beyond such monumental as well as small premises, he wrote over three hundred books regarding Buddhism and his philosophy of life. Accolades were too many to list.

Hsing Yun advocated Buddhism for mankind, thus he often made his teachings as simple and brief as possible, usually highly relevant to our daily living and easy to practice. His often-repeated motto was simplified into four-fold; to give others faith, happiness, hope, and convenience. These were mentioned again in his last will, disclosed after his death.

My first meeting with Monk Hsing Yun was rather ceremonious, at a gathering of over a thousand nuns, monks and spectators among his followers in November 2013. It took place at a huge auditorium in Taipei. Entering the stage in a wheel chair, the monk, then 88 years old, took special effort to stand up to hand me the Distinguished Life-time Achievement Award in Journalism.

This award, established for a number of years, was formerly given only to Taiwanese. I felt honored to be the first and only recipient from outside of Taiwan. I did not know of the nomination process before I was informed of being selected for the award, endowed with a rather large sum of prize money. I suspected my selection might be due to my decades of working on conservation of nature and culture, including restoration of several remote Buddhist monasteries and a nunnery. Many of these premises were in the Tibetan region of China where I had operated for decades. Following the announcement, a film crew was dispatched from Taiwan to Hong Kong to make an opening film regarding my rather modest achievements.

After the ceremony and a sumptuous meal, Monk Hsing Yun handed to me one of his famous calligraphy writings, mounted into a scroll. He also quietly urged me to use the award money on myself, rather than put it into the pool of funds in the non-profit organization that I had founded. I was glad to oblige, as I had little personal savings to my name. He further invited me to visit his main center in Fo Guang Shan in southern Taiwan.

Script to HM / 「行道天下」書法

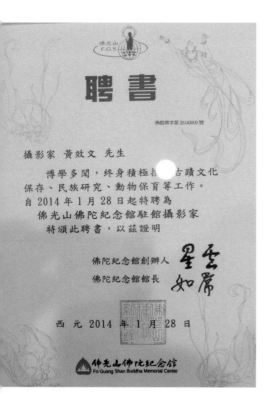

Appointment certificate / 「駐館攝影師」聘書

I took up his offer two months later, and ended up as his guest staying at a villa overlooking the grand towers and pavilions of Fo Guang Shan. He even personally introduced me to many of the latest buildings within the premises, all done to honor the Buddha, to whom he had dedicated his entire life since he was 14. I was able to roam the grounds and garden with him while pushing his wheelchair around as he enjoyed a leisurely and pleasant afternoon. Following us was a small entourage of nuns and a monk photographer to document my visit. During my stay, we had several wonderful vegetarian meals and tea breaks together.

In the evening, there was a gathering of a full auditorium of nuns when Monk Hsing Yun conferred on me yet another certificate, this time an appointment as Resident Artist in Photography for his Fo Guang Shan Buddhist Center. He revealed that such an appointment had only been given out once before, to Chinese Nobel Laureate Mo Yan, as Resident Artist in Literature. I felt both flattered and humbled.

As he had been photographed throughout his long career during many public functions, I asked that, as Resident Photographer, I should be allowed into his inner sanctuary and to photograph only his daily calligraphy exercise. The monk, always greeting me with a perpetual smile, at once heeded my request and asked his attending nuns to make

Gathering for appointment of HM / 聘任「駐館攝影師」的法會

arrangements for the following morning.

Next day, after an early breakfast, I was led to his simple but spacious home where Monk Hsing Yun was already seated. There was little on display except a very large green table with a velvet cloth over it, necessary for him to script his huge calligraphy. Usually, the monk was seen with his yellowish monk's robe. But this morning, he was dressed in his casual monk's rope in black, feeling fully at home. Thus began my several sessions of photographing the monk in action, documenting the scripting of his famous "One-Brush" calligraphy during my subsequent visits.

My first request that day was for him to script "when drinking water, think about the source" to complement my having been to several river sources in China, foremost of which were the sources of the Yangtze, Mekong and Yellow River.

"Drinking water think about the source" / 「飲水思源」

Monk Hsing Yun explained to me why his calligraphy was called "One-stroke brush". Due to decades of suffering from diabetes, he had lost ninety percent of his eyesight, and it was still deteriorating. Thus, if he stopped his brush stroke with one character, he might not know where to start the next, unable to align the characters into a vertical straight line. Therefore, he had to continue his writing as if they were all a single action stroke. The four characters scripted for me perfectly demonstrated this process.

He lived up to his motto by honoring my numerous requests, scripting the single word "Crane" for our crane exhibit, "Flying" for our aviation exhibit, "Zen" for our meditation premises at the Bodhidharma Cave. These calligraphies were all mounted and put on display at their appropriate places.

Perhaps the final photography session was the most memorable, something that illustrated Monk Hsing Yun's abidance to his motto of giving others convenience. I arrived again and requested to photograph him in action - writing action. But it was not to be, as by then he had been ill, in and out of hospital often. His upper arm had developed infection resulting with joint inflammation from over exercising his writing. His calligraphy had been used for years by his Buddhist order to raise money from his followers and the public at large. But he would not be writing anymore.

Still, in order to answer my wishes, he again invited me into his home. A pair of written scripts were already laid at the table with him seated in front of them. He asked his attending nun to produce his very large brush. With that in hand, he posed and imitated the position as if he had just finished writing the paired scripts. Upon my snapping a few shots, he took up the two scripts and offered them to me as final gifts.

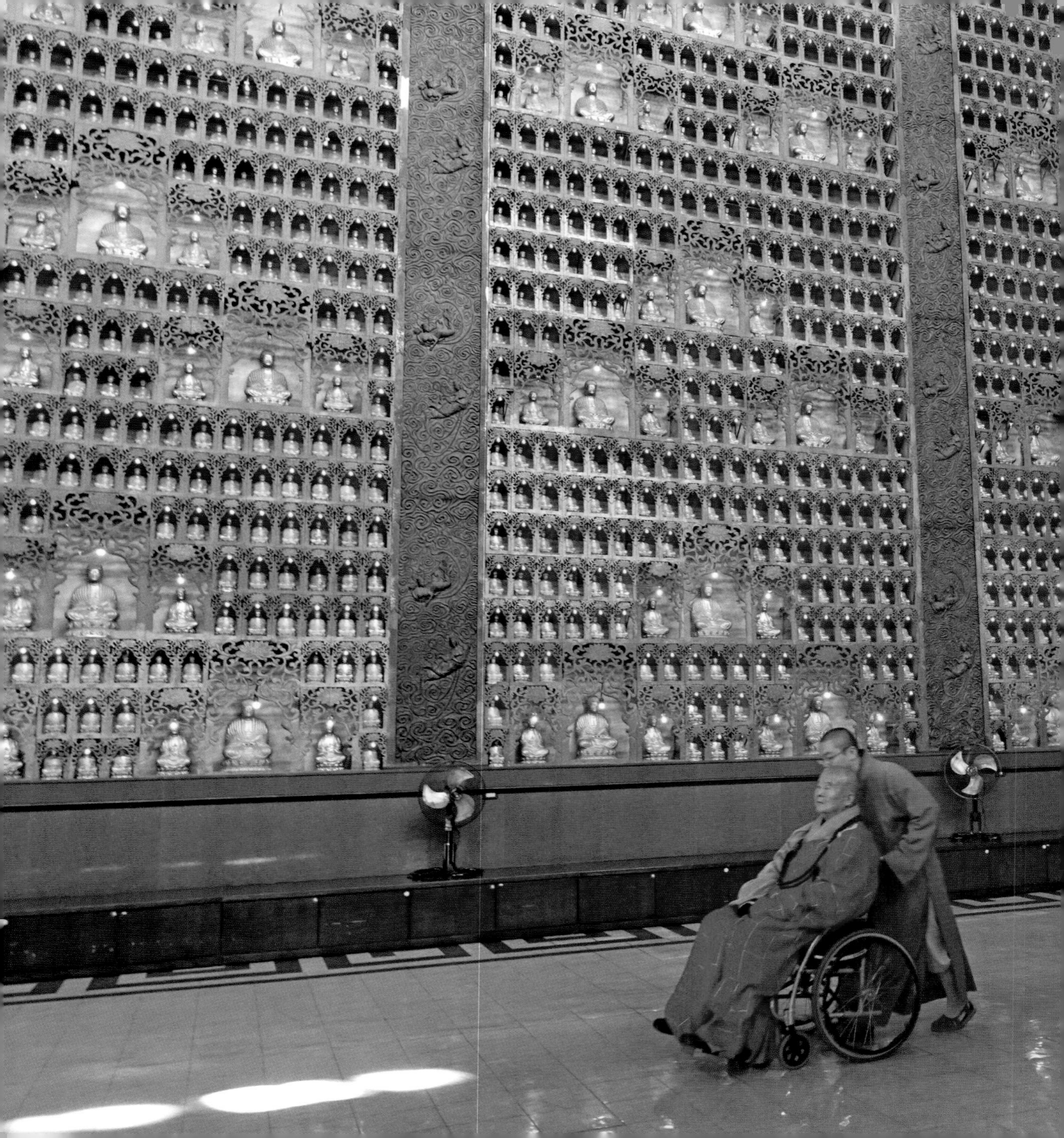

That evening, a nun showed up at my lodging villa. She presented two brush pens to me as a parting gift from Monk Hsing Yun. The large one was for writing, the smaller one for signing his iconic signature. Today, those two brushes are framed and on display at our small yet selective exhibition house in Hong Kong.

Remembering Monk Hsing Yun's four mottos, I feel highly honored and humbled to have received fully his last motto, "giving others convenience". Now the challenge will be for me to carry that motto onward.

Hsing Yun at big hall of statues / 星雲大師在佛殿

緣起星雲

點滴的瞬間

二〇二三年二月五日，星雲大師在台灣圓寂，享年九十七歲。當成千上萬的弟子和信徒在哀悼這位大師的離開時，我想藉此回憶一些我與這位生活簡單的僧人度過的點滴瞬間。

星雲大師是華人世界知名的僧人。他生前，在世界各地建立了兩百多所宗教中心，深受全球信徒的敬仰和尊重。而除這些宏偉或至微小的建築之外，他還撰寫了超過三百多本關於佛教以及個人人生哲學的書籍，被授予的榮譽更是數不勝數。

星雲大師畢生為人們弘揚佛法，他的教義往往簡單、扼要，和我們的日常生活息息相關，容易實踐。他那些最喜歡重複的人生信條可以簡化成四個部分：給人信心，給人歡喜，給人希望，給人方便。這些在他離世後公布的遺囑中也再次被提及。

我與星雲大師的第一次會面相當隆重。二〇一三年十一月，我被告知獲得「星雲終身成就獎」，到台北去領授我的獎狀和榮譽。頒獎儀式在台北的一個大禮堂進行，包括星雲大師和將近一千多名尼姑、僧人和觀眾。當時，這位已經八十八歲高齡的大師坐著輪椅上台，努力地站起來，將「新聞事業終身成就獎」的證書頒到我手上。

Hsing Yun standing to give award / 被星雲大師頒授獎狀　　Hsing Yun rising to his feet / 頒獎典禮上的星雲大師

其實，這個獎項在台灣已經設立多年，此前僅授予台灣本地。我非常榮幸地成為迄今為止第一也是唯一的台灣以外的獲獎者。在被授予這個殊榮之前，我並未被告知我被提名的程序，也不知道將被賦予一大筆獎金。我懷疑這是因為我數十年來一直致力於保護自然與文化，其中就包括修復幾座偏遠地區的佛教寺廟和一所尼姑庵。這些寺廟多半位於中國的青藏高原地區，我在那裡已經工作了幾十年的時間。自我被公布獲獎後，台灣的一個攝影團隊還專門到香港來，記錄我微小而綿薄的工作，以作為頒獎禮的開幕片。

在頒獎禮一頓豐富的晚餐之後，星雲大師遞給我一幅他的書法作品四字「行道天下」，精心地置放在一個卷軸中，我感覺當之有愧。他還悄悄勸我把獎金用在自己身上，而不是放在我創立的非牟利組織的資金池裡。這個建議被我欣然接受，因為我的名下並沒有多少私人的存款。隨後，他還邀請我去參觀了他在台灣南部佛光山的主要中心。

Hsing Yun greeting children / 星雲大師和小朋友
Hising Yun facing big Buddha / 星雲大師與大佛

距離頒獎典禮兩個月後，我受到星雲大師的邀請，以貴賓的身分住到了佛光山一座能夠俯瞰其宏偉塔樓和亭台樓閣的「紫竹林」別墅裡。星雲大師親自帶我參觀和介紹園區內新修的建築。他自十五歲起就將自己的一生奉獻給了佛陀，這些建築都是為了紀念佛陀而建造的。午後，我陪著星雲大師在花園和庭院裡散步，由我推著他的輪椅，讓他享受一個悠閒而愉快的下午。跟在我們後邊的是一群尼姑和一位僧人攝影師，悉心記錄著我的到訪。在此期間，我和星雲大師一起享用了佛光山美味的齋飯和茶歇。

這天傍晚，我還參加了一個超過一千多名尼姑和一百名和尚的盛大法會，法會後我被授予另外一個獎項，成為佛光山佛教中心的駐館攝影藝術家。據星雲大師透露，這樣的榮譽此前只賦予過獲得諾貝爾文學獎的中國作家莫言，以佛光山駐山作家的身分。我感到又自豪又受寵若驚。

在他漫長的職業生涯中，星雲大師的很多公共瞬間都被攝像機捕捉和記錄。作為佛光山的駐山攝影師，我大膽請求大師能夠允許我進入他的內殿，跟蹤拍攝他練習書法的日常。這位總是面帶微笑、和藹可親的僧人，當即答應了我的請求，並讓尼姑們開始為第二天做準備。

第二天早餐後，我被帶到大師簡樸而寬敞的居處兼書房，星雲大

師已經在那裡等候。房間裡無甚裝飾，除了一張非常大的綠色桌子，上面蓋著天鵝絨布，以方便大師書寫巨大的書法。通常，星雲大師都是穿著他黃色的僧袍。這天早上，他罕見地穿著褐色的僧侶便服，感受在家的自在。於是，我開始用相片拍攝和記錄大師著名的「一筆字」書法時刻。

那天，我的第一個請求是請大師幫我寫下「飲水思源」四個字，以致意我在中國幾個河流源頭的工作，其中最重要的是長江、湄公河和黃河源頭。

隨後星雲大師為我解釋了他的書法為什麼叫「一筆字」。因為長期受糖尿病的折磨，大師的雙眼已經失去了百分之九十的視力，並且在持續惡化。因此，如果他的毛筆停留在一個字的筆觸上，他就

"Contented lotus" / 「知足蓮」書法

Hsing Yun & HM / 星雲大師與我

Hsing Yun at home with HM / 星雲大師和我在他居處

不知道從哪裡開始第二筆，無法將文字對齊成垂直的直線。所以無論是一個字還是若干字，他都力求能夠一筆連續完成，一氣呵成。而為我書寫的這四個字恰好記錄了這個過程。

大師啟世的信條也完美地兌現在我的身上。在我的請求之下，星雲大師繼續為我們的黑頸鶴展覽贈予「鶴」字，為航空飛行展覽贈予「飛」字，以及為我們的達摩祖師洞閉關中心贈予「禪」字。現在，這些書法都被完好裱裝，存放在它們適當的位置。

這其中最令人難忘的，也最能體現大師「給人方便」信條的時刻，是我的最後一次拜訪。當我再次請求拍攝大師的書法，並獲贈墨寶時，負責丘尼告訴我星雲大師已生病多時，經常進出醫院。因為過度練習書法，星雲大師的上臂出現感染，導致骨關節發炎。大師的書法多年來一直被他的佛教中心用來募捐和籌集善款。但他暫時也不能寫作了。

"Crane" / 「鶴」　　　　　　　　　　　　　　　　　　　　"Fly" / 「飛」

儘管如此，為了滿足我的期望，星雲大師還是邀請我到他的住所。我到時，大師已經端坐在書房裡，面前是兩張已經寫好的書法。為了不讓我失望，他讓侍從拿出他那支很大的毛筆。拿著它，擺出提筆的姿勢，佯裝才剛剛完成了眼前的書法。我抓拍了幾張，隨後大師拿起那兩幅字畫，把它們當做最後的禮物送給了我。

那天傍晚，一個尼姑來到我居住的別墅。作為臨別的禮物，她送來了星雲大師給我的一對毛筆。大的是寫書法用的，小的用來簽他標誌性的簽名。現在，這兩支毛筆已經被裱裝起來，陳列在我們香港小而精緻的展覽館裡。

在星雲大師的四則信條中，我深感榮幸且謙卑地領惠到了大師的最後一個信條——「給人方便」。現在，留給我的挑戰是繼續秉承並把這個信條不斷發揚下去。

"Zen" / 「禪」

Gift to HM / 送給 HM 的禮物

北
海
道
冬
季
朝
聖

HOKKAIDO WINTER PILGRIMAGE

Tsurui, Hokkaido - February 17, 2023

HOKKAIDO WINTER PILGRIMAGE
Nature & Wildlife

A world dressed in white with an undulating line of naked trees has a very special appeal to my eyes and mind. Nature always offers a humbling reality check for my otherwise inflated ego. Wrapped in heavy down clothing from head to toe allows me to stay out in the open for some reasonable length of time to appreciate this pristine and serene ecosystem. Hokkaido sits atop the rest of Japan like a jeweled crown.

The chill to my face, the only exposed skin, cuts a penetrating path to my brain and makes me think more acutely. Suddenly, other functional work and social obligations are left behind and dissipate, like the steam rising from the hot spring when I take off layers of clothes and soak myself.

The spring by Lake Kussharo is so natural that even naming it seems contaminating. Two tiny wooden huts, one for men, the other women, are available for changing, or rather undressing. Steps away, over snow with bare feet and bare body, are two open-air pools somewhat hidden among a few big rocks. At best, they could fit half a dozen on each side. Half a dozen human bathers, yet usually no one is there. As for geese and ducks, several dozens of these wild birds are the perpetual winter residents right up to the pools, enjoying the discharged warmth of the hot spring.

Isolated among nature, with distant greyish forests anchored in whitish snow, any burden and worries, even happy moments and thoughts, are a world away. I first came to Kushiro in 2010 to seek out the Red-crowned Crane. By then, I had already worked on and photographed their cousins, the Black-necked Crane of the Tibetan plateau for over twenty years. Since then, eastern Kushiro has become my annual winter hide-out for cleansing of body and mind. The pandemic interrupted this ritual with a three-year hiatus, which I am now able to break.

As I got out of the pool, an elderly Japanese man arrived to take his bath. Buses have just arrived to end my morning courtship with nature. Internet and mobile phone now have made this distant hot spring enclave a tourist stop - a hot dot on any Google map for those seeking a selfie. Swarms of photographic freaks will take up the lakefront, creating a human cordon between the nature bathers and the nature flyers.

Cameras will click away like machine guns spraying bullets, though the birds will take little notice and not fall with the shots nor take flight. They are now used to these camera-lugging armies with long lenses and tripods, and should feel fortunate that these are not real guns. In fact, some of the infantry may even cast grains to feed them, compromising their natural instinct of foraging for themselves.

HM in winter gear / 全副武裝的 HM
Geese and ducks by hot spring / 溫泉旁的野鳥

Japanese bather / 日本浴客
Winter scene / 冬天雪景

Perhaps due to my long career of a half century as a photojournalist, shooting positive slides until 2006 when I belatedly turned digital, I have always treated my camera shutter with respect and pride. Respect, in that film was always considered a limited resource, and pride, in that a careful snap resulting in the perfect image that I aspired to get could be most gratifying. Though my first Nikon F1 came with motor-drive, I never used it for multiple shots, and took on each shot with care, though swift and deliberate.

The joy I derive from photographing cranes in flight, especially pairing ones, is most delightful. Shooting cranes on the ground, even dancing ones, has become so mundane as to produce no challenge at all. I often wonder why, with today's advancement in cameras and lenses, auto-focus and anti-vibration mode, high ISO settings to compensate for high f-stop for depth of field while offering fast exposure speed, photographers still care to use, or "wear", super heavy long lenses with fully camouflaged outer coating. Such clumsy outfits, especially mounted to tripods, prohibit fast camera action in following the cranes in action or in flight. I continue to opt for a perfectly adequate Nikon D850 with only a light-weight 28-300 zoom lens.

As with the Steller's Sea Eagle - with its huge golden beak, its gliding in flight is the most majestic image to capture, with occasional intertwining

HM in hot spring / HM 在泡溫泉

Roosting cranes / 棲息的鶴群

Cranes in flight / 飛行中的鶴群

Cranes in flight / 飛行中的鶴群

with the White-tailed Sea Eagle. Such moments make it well worth the effort, leaving the house at 5 AM for a three-hour drive to the coast, followed by braving the cold sea wind on a ferry boat. The results again speak for themselves.

On the last day in Hokkaido, I took a two-hour drive to coastal Notsuke, a narrow prawn-shaped peninsula. This is where I have in the past come in close contact with red fox and plenty of antlered deer. Perhaps good karma would follow me once again.

As I drove to the mid-point of the peninsula towards the lighthouse at the end, a red fox in full winter coat came out from the snow-bank onto the road. It sat momentarily to block me from driving forward. Looking intently into my eyes, she (it must be a female) gracefully strolled back to the snow-bank. There she sat casually and gave me a glance with a twinkle in her eyes.

From that barely three-meter distance, she began posing in front of my camera, sitting, rising, and walking back and forth as if doing her catwalk or foxtrot. Imagined or real, it doesn't really matter, as I cherished this very special moment of romantic courtship with this very lovely furred beauty.

Camera-freaks / 攝影愛好者們

北海道冬季朝聖

自然與野生動物之美

現在這裡是一片披上白紗的世界，連綿的枯樹好像海上的波浪起伏蜿蜒其間。這樣的景緻總是能喚起我最感性的審美。大自然的力量能讓不知天高地厚的人虛心接受現實的「冷酷」，就像此刻，我正將自己包裹在厚重冬裝中，從頭到腳都穿得嚴嚴實實，這樣我才能在戶外多待，然後再多待一會兒，去欣賞這片未經玷汙、寧靜祥和的純白世界。這裡是北海道，日本島之上的瑰麗皇冠，瑰麗皇冠上最璀璨的那顆明珠。

即使只露了出一點臉部皮膚，凜冽的寒風帶來的冰冷感還是直衝我的腦門，使我思緒更加敏銳。剎那間，現實世界帶來的一切複雜的責任、義務，統統都被拋在腦後，就好像當我脫掉層層衣物，浸泡在溫泉中時，它們就隨著蒸汽升騰，飄散而去。

屈斜路湖畔的泉水是如此純淨，以至於為它命名似乎都會汙染它的自然本色。兩座小小的木屋靜靜佇立，分別供男士和女士更衣，或者更貼切地說是「脫衣」。幾步之外，赤腳裸身跨過鋪滿雪的地面，就到了兩處露天溫泉池，隱密在幾塊巨石之間。每邊最多只能容納五六個浴客同時泡湯，然而通常是無人享用的。有幾十隻野雁和鴨子是溫泉池邊的永久冬日居民，享受著這片泉水散發出的溫暖。

在大自然的孤絕之中，遠處灰白交錯的森林深處，所有的負擔和憂慮，甚至歡樂的時

刻和思緒，都像是無比遙遠的事，遙遠到不值一提。我初次來到釧路是在二○一○年，為了尋找丹頂鶴。那時，我已經花了二十多年的時間在西藏高原研究和紀錄牠們的近親——黑頸鶴。自那以後，釧路東部成為了我每年冬季淨化身心的祕密基地。新冠疫情讓我和我的定期治癒之旅闊別了三年，現在，我終於得以再次回到這裡。

當我走出泉池，一位年長的日本男士正好準備進來接我的班。第一班公車載著遊客剛剛抵達，結束了我與大自然的晨間私語。顯然，網際網路和手機已經讓這個遙遠的溫泉村成了 *Google* 地圖上的熱門打卡點。大批攝影發燒友佔據了湖岸，好像一條橫亙在我們這些赤身裸體的浴者和丹頂鶴之間的天然警戒線。

Lake Kussharo / 屈斜路湖

Fox wink / 來自赤狐的媚眼

Foxtrot / 赤狐踱步

Ural Owl / 長尾林鴞
White-tailed eagle / 白尾海鵰
Steller's sea eagle / 虎頭海鵰

照相機的快門聲好像機關槍噴射子彈一樣誇張，然而鳥兒們並不在意，不會隨著快門聲「倒下」或飛走。牠們現在已經習慣了這些背著相機、帶著長鏡頭和三腳架的「軍團」。或許牠們還應該慶幸這些人背著的不是真槍實彈，畢竟軍團中的一些「步兵」有時還會撒下糧食來投餵牠們，但是其實這樣做反而會削弱牠們自力覓食的自然本能。

作為一名職涯長達半個世紀的攝影記者，我直到二〇〇六年才轉向數碼拍攝，或許正因如此，我始終對我的相機快門抱有尊重和自豪。尊重之心，源於我一直將膠卷視為珍貴有限的資源；自豪則來自於，每一次細心的拍攝，我都力求捕捉到滿足自我要求的完美影像，所以由此而帶來的滿足感是最令我喜悅的。我從來不會盲目地進行連拍，每一次，我都是腦袋先想好，眼睛隨後，手再按下快門。

在空中飛翔的鶴，尤其是成雙成對飛行的鶴，是近年來我最沉迷於拍攝的對象。拍攝地面上的鶴，即便是牠在跳舞，與我而言失去了挑戰性。我常常好奇，為何在今天這個攝像技術和鏡頭工藝大幅進步、自動對焦和防震模式俱全，高感光度可補償高光圈以獲得景深，同時提供快速曝光速度的時代，攝影師們仍然選擇使用笨重又穿戴著迷彩外衣的超長鏡頭。這種笨拙的裝備，尤其還被安裝在三腳架上，怎麼能捕捉到擁有超快移動速度的野鶴

呢？我反正會繼續用我那台焦距 28-300 的 Nikon D850，完全夠用而且輕量。

虎頭海鵰有著巨大的金黃鳥喙，在空中滑翔時很是雄偉颯爽。偶爾，我還能捕捉到牠與白尾海鵰盤旋交錯的情景，每每這種時刻，我都覺得清晨五點離家，驅車三小時到海岸，然後在渡船上忍受冰冷的海風，這些所有的努力都是值得的。成果總是會不言自明。

在北海道的最後一天，我驅車兩小時到達海岸邊的野付，那是一個狹長的舌形半島。在這裡，我曾與赤狐和許多大角鹿不期而遇。我祈禱著這次好運也會伴隨著我。

我的目的地是半島末端的燈塔，行至半途，突然有隻全身厚毛的赤狐從路邊的雪堆中緩緩走出來。牠在道中間短暫地坐了一會，攔住了我的去路。我猜她肯定是個雌性，因為她退場時深深地凝視了我一眼，然後優雅地回到雪堆那邊，慵懶地盤坐在地，用眼中閃爍的光芒再次給我投來一瞥。

隨後，她開始在我的鏡頭前擺姿勢，坐下、站起、踱步，彷彿在進行她的時尚走秀。此時，我們的距離只有三公尺。夢境與現實在此刻彼此模糊也無關緊要，因為我正沉醉於與這位毛茸茸的美麗女士共度的，珍貴的浪漫瞬間。

Fox in front of car / 停在我車前的赤狐
Deer / 鹿

緬懷曹中越

REMEMBERING CAO ZHONGYUE
(1966 – 2023)

REMEMBERING CAO ZHONGYUE (1966 – 2023)

Cao Zhongyue, fondly called Xiao Cao by us, first joined CERS in 1993, driving our two newly imported Land Rovers from Kunming to Lhasa. From that time, he was with CERS continually for thirty years.

Xiao Cao was released from China's PLA after participating in the final battles with Vietnam along the China/Vietnam border. He then joined the Yunnan Institute of Geography, at the time CERS's partner in research and conservation in the remotest parts of China. Starting as a driver with mechanical skills acquired during his service in the army, useful for car repair, Cao became also my back-up videographer.

Cao was by my side on expeditions to all six of the river sources that CERS defined. These included the Yangtze, Mekong, Yellow River, Salween, Irrawaddy and Brahmaputra. Pictures of him at each of these sources now stand as memorials to his expeditionary achievements. He further provided logistic support for our caving team, and he was at the forefront of much of our research and conservation work on the Black-necked Crane, Tibetan Antelope, Wild Yak, Snub-nosed Monkey, and many other species.

Beyond China, Xiao Cao also traveled with me to Myanmar and Palawan in the Philippines multiple times, always ready to help and lend a hand beyond the call of duty. I remember well all his support and contributions to CERS and to me personally. Our last field trip outside of China was into the border region of upper Myanmar near Tibet. Even during the pandemic, he escorted me through countless roadblocks into and out of Tibet.

As the driver/manager of the large fleet of CERS cars, handling everything from routine registration to minute repairs and spare-parts inventory for intricate and demanding expeditions, Xiao Cao never missed a beat. With him in charge, I always felt well assured. And his video record of our work is now an important and integral part of our film archive.

Arjin Shan Nature Reserve, Cao on right / 右邊是曹中越，阿爾金山保護區

Xiao Cao's most important project and perhaps his lasting legacy, however, is that he helped me design, and then single-handedly organized building and management of our meditation premises at the sacred Damozhong, or Bodhidharma Cave, a very important pilgrimage site in northwest Yunnan.

Xiao Cao, as member of the CERS team, circumambulated the most sacred Mount Kailash twice, in 2002 and 2018, gaining merit that would accompany him into his next life. We mourn his passing, way too early, but cherish what he has left with us from his thirty years of service to CERS. We, who now carry on in what should have been his remaining years, should make best use of the time that he left with us to carry our work forward.

Cao to Yangtze source 1995 / 曹中越在長江源頭 1995 年
With new born Tibetan Antelope 1998 / 新生藏羚羊 1998 年
Western Tibet 1999 / 西藏西部 1999 年

Cao far left, Khampa fighters 1997 / 曹在最左，康巴戰士 1997 年

緬懷曹中越（一九六六 — 二〇二三）

曹中越，我們都親切地稱呼他為小曹。自從一九九三年，他駕駛著我們嶄新的兩輛進口路虎車從昆明進到拉薩，就正式加入學會，到現在已經三十年了。

小曹從過軍，參加過中越邊境自衛反擊戰中越南戰役的最後戰鬥。從中國人民解放軍復原後，他加入了當時在中國最偏遠地區和學會在研究和保護領域有著深厚合作關係的雲南地理研究所。從一開始的駕駛員，用他在部隊服役時掌握的一些機械技能修護車輛，到後來逐漸成為了我的輔助攝影師。

在學會的六次大型的江河源頭的野外探險考察中，小曹和我一直都是並肩同行。這些河流包括長江、湄公河、黃河、薩爾溫江、伊洛瓦底江和雅魯藏布江。他在這些源頭拍攝的每張照片，都是他遠征成就的勳章。除此之外，他還為我們洞穴探險隊的隊員提供了充足的後勤保障。在我們對黑頸鶴、藏羚羊、野犛牛、金絲猴和許多其他物種的研究和保護工作中，他總是走在最前面。

除中國以外，我和小曹還多次一同前往緬甸和菲律賓的巴拉望，除去日常工作，他總是細心主動地為大家提供幫助。我清楚的記得他為學會和我個人給予的支持和貢獻。我們最後一次出境野外考察是在靠近西藏邊境的緬甸。即使在疫情期間，他也曾護送

我穿越無數路障，進出西藏。

作為學會大型車隊的駕駛員和主要負責人，小曹總是用心地處理著和車輛相關的所有日常工作，包括細微維護和檢修，以及複雜而嚴苛的探險裝備備份和庫存的事宜。任何細節都逃不過他的眼睛，有他負責，我總是感到很放心。而他為野外工作拍攝的影片材料，都是我們素材庫裡重要的影像資料。

然後這其中最重要，也是小曹最為不朽的遺產，或許是他幫助我設計，並一手組織、建造和管理的位於雲南西北部一個非常重要的佛教朝聖地，達摩祖師洞的閉關中心。

作為（香港）中國探險學會的一員，小曹在二〇〇二年和二〇一八年兩年，曾先後完成兩次岡仁波齊神山的轉山之旅，從中積累了他下世輪迴中的善業和功德。我們如今哀悼他的離世，但他在學會三十年間的付出和奉獻是永恆的。在餘下的時間裡，讓我們藉著小曹精神，再一起繼續向前。

Hanging coffins 1999 / 懸掛棺木 1999 年

Dege Sichuan 1994 / 四川 德格 1994 年
Yunnan caving / 雲南洞穴探險

Snub-nosed Monkey 2002 / 金絲猴 2002 年
Kailash 2002 / 岡仁波齊神山 2002 年

以
海
為
家

AT HOME WHILE AT SEA

El Nido, Palawan – March 13, 2023

AT HOME WHILE AT SEA
Exploring Palawan north

As soon as we leave port, the flying fish dart off left and right into the distance as our bow cuts through an otherwise calm sea off Tiniguiban of El Nido. We are heading for Coron, an archipelago of islands off the northern tip of Palawan. It is yet another dream come true. Over the last eight or nine years, I have explored much of Palawan, from south to north and east to west. What remains is Coron, beyond the northern tip of the main island.

We had just boarded the outrigger boat during low tide at the predawn hour of 5:30, ferrying our loads of luggage, food supplies, and passengers two at a time on a tiny kayak, crossing back and forth for a hundred meters distance to our boat. This double-outrigger boat, Mart Ace 2, with Captain Julius and three as crew, will be our home for the following four days out at sea. My team is seven: my ADC Berry, Jocelyn our Palawan site manager, Tsomo my Tibetan RA, Lisa the assistant cook, and two Batak boys from our site to help as deck hands. Thus, there are 11 of us on the boat. As we set sail, the much-anticipated sunrise over the horizon is just around the corner.

Once on the open sea and watching the boat's bow rising and falling with the surf, my mind likewise goes through hikes and drops. I marvel at nature's immensity while feeling humbled by our tiny existential being. Having my tan-top on should allow me to go home with some compensation in bragging rights. Hopefully this tan will trump friends returning from Phuket or Bali; my south sea tan like the famous south sea pearls, cultivated around the pristine sea of Palawan.

To quench my thirst in the pristine crystal-clear water, we make multiple island hops on the very first day: Takling, Calibangbang, Cobra, Cala-Cala, Cagdanao and finally Balenben where we stop for the night. All these islands have pristine coral reefs where I make haste to jump in and snorkel. But soon my memory of each starts blurring one into the other. Yet I remember well the first stop at Takling when I dived in with my new snorkel. Bogs, the most active among the crew and son of the owner of our boat, jumped in to guide me along. At 21, he is attending college in hotel and tourism study at PPS, but has taken off a few days to come home and accompany us to sea.

As we were snorkeling close to shore, Bogs suddenly surfaced and called out to the boat for help. He saw an octopus on the bottom and was hastily asking for the spear gun to be brought over while he followed the fast-crawling multi-legged animal below. Julius jumped off with the gun and soon was at the scene. I watched helplessly as the duo dived in and out of the water, trying to corner this smart aleck before his jet of ink hid his

Sunrise from boat / 船上日出
Julius captaining our boat / 船長朱利亞斯

whereabouts. It took about half a minute, then I saw Julius raise his steel dart with the octopus attached to its head. With its tentacles stretching up to a meter long, this would be barbecued fresh to supplement our dinner.

The first night we stop at Balenben, to be our base camp. There is a small Catholic church here serving the island's total of thirty households, with about 100 people. Nilo Sumayo is 48 and his wife Laylanie own the camp, along with his wife's four siblings. In 2014, the family invested and built small huts at the camp site on land belonging to Laylanie's mother. After three years of construction, the campsite opened in 2017, hosting guests from Europe, America and even China.

Before the pandemic, during peak season, they could host around thirty guests each night with a total of 13 rooms. The campsite is in business from October to June, making an average profit of 50,000 pesos every month. Their profit is shared evenly amongst the siblings. We take up three tiny A-frame thatched huts, barely large enough to set up a mosquito net over a sleeping pad. It

Full meal on boat / 船上的饕餮盛宴

No-eye-see 1000 perso/3 fish / 一千三條魚貴到不忍直視

costs 300 peso each for one night, while the others stay on the boat.

Nilo is from a neighboring area called Bray New Culaylayan. He started working there for a Japanese-owned oyster and pearl farming company in 2001. In 2005, he met his wife and they got married in 2006. Nilo and his wife have three children, two daughters and a son. Nilo has worked at the oyster and pearl farm for twenty-two years and is planning to retire soon when he reaches fifty years old. Oyster and pearl cultivation usually takes about sixteen to eighteen months before harvesting. They currently harvest the pearls four times a year. This Japanese company has a dozen such farms around Palawan.

The next day involves more island hopping; Bulawit, San Miguel, Demansing; until we arrive at Araw Beach of Culion Island, now truly a part of Coron. Here we set up tents on the beach and observe a most beautiful sunset as outrigger fishing boats sail out to sea for their night's catch during the squid season. In between, we run into a mega yacht, probably around 50 meters in length, at anchor at a wonderful beach. A few gentlemen with young ladies are seated under a specially set up cabana. They seem to have a few bodyguards within respectable distance of them. I, however, feel we are having a more care-free time with our outrigger yacht.

HM with octopus shot / HM 與章魚

Sally Cruz and her husband Raymond Cruz own a small convenience store and fish shop in Araw Beach. Sally is 40 years old, and her husband Raymond Cruz is 41. The couple have three teenage children. The young couple invested 10,000 pesos to open the convenience store and the fish shop. Every night, Raymond can catch around 9 kilos of squid and fish, earning an average income of 50,000 peso every month.

There is no government restriction on fishing in the Araw Beach area, so Raymond can go fishing whenever the weather is nice. When he catches fish or squid, he stores them in the ice box and then transports them to Manila to sell in the seafood market. Usually, a big fish (50cm or more) costs about 50 pesos per half-kilo, while the smaller fish (20cm) costs about 100 pesos, worth almost twice the larger catch. When the villagers nearby catch fish, they too would come to sell their fresh catch to Raymond. Usually, for a small fish between 20cm~25cm long he would pay about 100 pesos per fish.

Bogs, my young guide, comes from the larger district village of Linapacan. We call at its "port" while an antiquated wooden boat "Manila" is being loaded with foam boxes of seafood filled with ice. They will start the slow, thirty-hour journey to Manila shortly. Many other passengers are climbing in through the windows with their luggage. Looking at the age of this boat, I can only hope that the sea stays calm.

While I am still admiring the coral growing up to the pier with plenty of fish around our docked boat, Bogs rushes home and comes over with a transport motor tricycle. We board the side carriage, somewhat like a cage, which is usually used for livestock like pigs and chicken. Bogs drives us along the short coastal road, and within a couple kilometers, the cement road narrows to barely wide enough for our tricycle before ending where construction is still under way. In between, we stop to look at an enclave with limestone hill and sea cave. It was here, Bogs says, that some Japanese soldiers hid after the war ended.

Returning to town, we visit Bogs's family and meet his parents. His father Razel Militar owns two tourist boats and his mother and sisters operate a village store attached to their home. Towards the other end of the village the road also comes to a dead end. Here, there are women fetching drinking water from a very historical well, situated amazingly near the waterfront. There is a long line-up of water containers, as each family waits their turn to get water from the well. Nearby, other women are washing their clothes, but carved above the well are huge letters prohibiting anyone from bathing or washing clothes in the well.

Most islands we stop at have few families. Larger ones may have a school and one or more churches. Generally these villages are clean and simple. But one stands out as exception, as its name announces. Bulok Bulok phonetically in Philippines means "Rotten Rotten", and this small island village is Bulok Bulokan. The houses are indeed in rotten condition; many

Island fish vender / 島上的魚販
Sea Turtle / 偶遇海龜

Camping at Araw Beach / 在阿勞海灘紮營

Mart Ace 2 boat / 我們移動的家

Vince's villa / 文斯的別墅
Cathedral spire by nature / 鬼斧神工般的教堂塔尖

seem half-abandoned. The two newest structures are a very large, covered, government-built sports court and a small bamboo arena used as a staging area for cock fights.

At the time of our visit, the sports court is hosting multiple games, all at the same time. Four teams, two on each side, play on two ends of the basketball court. The middle ground is hosting a volleyball game, while a few younger kids are rolling rubber wheels around the court.

Rico is 54 and seated in the shade when I climb a dilapidated wooden ladder to get onto the jetty. He is using his knife to ply open cashews to get the nuts out for sale. Under the sun are more cashews being dried. I can tell from his slightly injured index fingers that his knife must be sharp. Likewise, his mind is sharp, as he tells the story behind the name Bulok Bulok.

Once this island and its surrounding sea had plenty of octopus. The locals would catch them and send them to distant markets for sale. But this was before the motorized age, so when they got to market, the octopus would all be rotten. Thus the island was given the name Bulok Bulok. Today, the octopus are no more, but the name has stuck. Before parting, Rico tells me that he has two pieces of waterfront land for sale in an island opposite

Bulok Bulok. But given the distance and the current rotten state of Bulok Bulok, they would likely remain on the market for some time to come.

On the third day, before arriving at Bulok Bulokan, we had stopped by other islands belonging to Culion; Pasyak Island, Tambon, Ditaytayan. But that night we spent the night sleeping on the boat, and I took up the upper deck and hard floor with no mat. By the fourth day, I feel I am fully toasted by the sun, since I never bother to use any sunblock on my skin. After all, my entire body has been seasoned for decades by UV at the extreme altitude of the Tibetan plateau.

My last dive is at Asis Island. As I swam to shore, I find a bushy sea anemone by my feet. Momentarily, four little Nemo come out, as if playing hide and seek among the anemone. That obviously makes my day, as I too have found Nemo.

I leave the boat, which has been my home away from home for four days, feeling like it has been much longer. Enjoying sunrise and sunset each day, with a long stretch in between, it has been as if time has come to a halt. We travel on to El Nido to spend two relaxing days at my friend Vince Perez's private villa on Helicopter Island.

The nearby limestone hills at a pristine lagoon are filled with edgy spine-like sculpture of nature. It reminds me of the ever-evolving Sagrada Familia Cathedral of Gaudi Barcelona, now into its 140 years of being built. A real shower will be a most welcomed finale to my short excursion to this south sea paradise. But the sweet memories will not be washed off for a long time to come.

以海為家

探索菲律賓巴拉望島北部

我們的船頭劃破了艾爾尼多島蒂尼吉班外海的寧靜海面。離港的航程中，船身的左右兩側，飛魚紛紛躍出水面，向遠方掠去。我們正前往科隆群島，它位於巴拉望島北端的外海。這又是一個夢想成真的時刻。在過去的八、九年間，我探索了巴拉望的大部分地區，從南到北，從東到西。現在，唯一剩下的就是主島北端的科隆。

凌晨五點半，我們剛剛在退潮時分登上了一艘雙體船。行李、食物和補給品都在一百米外，所以我們用一艘小皮划艇一次載兩個人，來回穿梭，將它們運送到我們船上。這艘名為「馬特艾斯 2 號」的雙體船將臨時充當我們未來四天海上之旅的家。船長叫朱利葉斯，船上還另有三名船員，而我的團隊共有七人：我的助理貝瑞、我們在巴拉望島的項目經理喬斯琳、我的藏族研究助理措莫、助理廚師麗莎，以及來自我們巴拉望基地的兩個巴塔克族男孩，他們將協助擔任甲板水手。因此，船上總共有我們十一個人。啟航時，太陽正從地平線上緩緩升起，我們就這樣與美景不期而遇。

航行於開闊的海面，看著船頭隨著波濤起伏，我的心緒也隨之跌宕。我對自然的浩瀚感到驚嘆，同時又因我們渺小的存在而感到謙卑。海上的豔陽打在我只穿著棕褐色背心的身體上，估計會讓我帶著一些值得炫耀的「成果」回家，比如一些晒痕，我覺得能勝過從普吉島或峇里島回來的朋友們。南海賜於我的黑色皮膚，就像著名的南海珍

珠，都是在巴拉望潔淨的海域中自然「培育」出來的。

為了看足這片美麗的海域，我們在第一天就跳了好幾個島：塔克林、卡利班班、科布拉、卡拉-卡拉、卡格達奈，最後在巴倫班島歇腳過夜。這些島嶼都擁有未受汙染的原始珊瑚礁，每到一處，我都會迫不及待地跳進水中浮潛。雖然不久後，我對每個島的記憶開始混合模糊，但是我能清楚地記得第一站塔克林。當時我戴著全新的浮潛裝備跳入水中，由船員中最活躍的波格斯引導我前行。波格斯是船長的兒子，二十一歲，在巴拉望公主港的大學學習酒店與旅遊管理，這次他特意抽出幾天時間回家，陪我們出海。

當我們在近岸浮潛時，波格斯突然浮出水面，大聲向船上求助。原來，他在海底看見了一隻章魚，於是急忙要求將魚叉槍帶過來，同時緊盯著那隻正快速溜走的章魚。隨後，朱利亞斯迅速跳下船趕到現場。我幫不上忙，所以只能在一旁看著他們潛入水中，試圖在章魚噴墨隱藏行踪之前將牠逼到角落。大約半分鐘後，朱利亞斯揚起了他收穫滿滿的鋼叉。那隻章魚的觸手竟長達一米，看來我們今晚的海鮮燒烤會更豐盛。

第一晚，我們停靠在巴倫班島，在這裡的一個營地裡安頓修整。這裡有一座小天主教堂，服務島上總共三十戶、約一百個居民。四十八歲的尼洛·蘇馬和他的妻子萊拉妮共同擁有這片營地，萊

Shuttling supplies to boat / 把補給品運上船

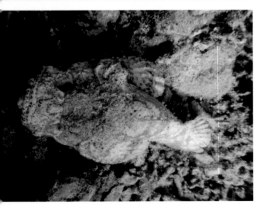

拉尼的四個兄弟姊妹也是股東。這片營地的土地所有權其實屬於萊拉尼的媽媽，二〇一四年，他們一家在這裡建造了幾個小木屋。經過三年的建設，營地於二〇一七年開放，接待來自歐洲、美國和中國的客人。

在新冠疫情之前的旺季，他們的十三個房間每晚能夠接待大約三十名客人。營區每年十月到六月開放，每月平均利潤為五萬披索，掙的錢兄弟姊妹之間均分。我們租了三間剛好能搭建蚊帳的尖頂型小茅草屋，空間小到只夠放一張地鋪和一個蚊帳。每人每晚花費三百披索，其他人則留在船上。

尼洛來自附近的一個名叫布雷新庫拉延的地方。他從二〇〇一年開始在一家日資牡蠣和珍珠養殖公司工作。他在二〇〇五年遇見了他的妻子，兩人在二〇〇六年結婚。尼洛和他的妻子有兩個女兒和一個兒子。現在，尼洛已經在牡蠣和珍珠養殖公司工作了二十二年，計畫在年滿五十歲時退休。牡蠣和珍珠通常需要大約十六到十八個月才能收穫，目前，他們每年能收四次珍珠。這家日本公司在巴拉望周圍有十幾個類似的養殖場。

Super yacht & us / 與超級遊艇合影
Bogs free diving / 波格斯在自由地潛水
White Stone Fish / 白色石狗公

隔天，我們繼續著跳島遊，探訪了更多島嶼，布拉威、聖米蓋、德曼興……直到抵達庫里恩島的阿勞海灘，才算真正踏上科隆群島的一部分。我們在這片海灘上搭建帳篷，觀賞著最美麗的日落，同時看著漁船在魷魚季出海，帶回一箱箱豐盛的戰利品。期間，我們遇到了一艘大約五十米長的超級遊艇，幾位紳士帶著年輕女士坐在他們自己搭的漂亮小亭下，似乎在禮貌的距離範圍內還有幾位保鏢護衛。這麼一對比，我覺得還是我們的小船更加無拘無束，自由自在。

薩莉・克魯茲和她的丈夫雷蒙德・克魯茲在阿勞海灘擁有一家小賣部和魚店。薩莉今年四十歲，她的丈夫雷蒙德・克魯茲四十一歲，共同養育三個正值青春期的小孩。小賣部和魚店是他們花了一萬披索換來的。每晚，雷蒙德可以捕捉大約九公斤的魷魚，每月平均收入五萬披索。

阿勞海灘不受政府限漁令的限制，所以雷蒙德碰到好天氣就可以自在地出海。當他捕到好魚時，就把牠們儲存到保冷箱然後運送到馬尼拉的海鮮市場賣掉。通常，一條五十公分或以上的大魚能賣到每半公斤五十披索，而二十公分或以下較小的魚售價約為每半公斤一百披索，幾乎是大魚的兩倍。有時附近的村民捕到新鮮好魚時也會賣給雷蒙德。通常，對於二十至二十五公分長的小魚，他會出價約一百披索每條。

我二十一歲的年輕嚮導波格斯出身於當地較大的農村利納帕坎。此時正有一艘老舊的木船「馬尼拉號」載著有冰鎮海鮮的保麗龍箱子停靠在這個村子的港口，雖然我不知道這麼小的區域能不能算做一個港口。片刻後，他們將開始緩慢漫長的，三十小時的旅程，目的地是馬尼拉。許多「乘客」正帶著行李從窗戶爬上船。看看這船的年紀，我只能希望海面保持平靜。

當我仍在欣賞碼頭邊瘋狂生長的珊瑚和周圍的魚群時，波格斯匆忙回家騎了一輛三輪車來。我們上

了邊上的側車廂，有點像籠子，感覺平時這裡應該是用來運像豬和雞等家畜的。波格斯載著我們沿著短短的沿海小道行駛，幾公里後，水泥路變窄到僅夠我們的三輪車通過，道路盡頭是一處仍在施工中的工地。中途我們在一座有石灰岩山丘和海邊洞穴的小島停留了一會。波格斯說，二戰結束後有些日本士兵就躲在這裡。

返回鎮上，我們拜訪了波格斯的家人。他的父親擁有兩艘觀光船，母親和姊妹們經營著他們家的村莊商店。通往村子另一端的路也是死路，靠近海邊有一口水井，井邊有排成一個長排的容器，每一個容器都代表一個家庭在此等待著取水。井口不遠處，還有些婦女正在洗衣服，但在井上方可刻著明顯的大字：禁止任何人在井裡沐浴及洗衣。

我們停靠的大多數島嶼都家庭稀少，較大的島上才會有一所學校或一兩座教堂。通常這些村莊都是乾淨簡樸的，但有一個例外，正如其名所宣告的那樣矚目。在菲律賓語中，「Bulok Bulok」音譯為「腐爛腐爛」，而這個小村莊就叫做 Bulok Bulokan。這裡的房屋確實都很破爛，許多看起來似乎半廢棄了。兩座最新的建築大得顯眼，而且是有屋頂的，一處是政府建造的運動場，另一處是用作鬥雞表演的竹製競技場。

我們造訪的時候，運動場正在同時舉辦多場比賽。四支隊伍，每邊兩隊，在籃球場的兩端進行比賽。中間地帶正在進行一場排球比賽，而一些年幼的孩子們正在場地周圍滾動著橡膠輪胎。

我爬上一個破舊的木梯，通過它上到了碼頭，此時五十四歲的瑞可正坐在碼頭陰涼處用刀子劈開腰果取出果仁來賣，一旁的陽光下還有很多他晾晒的腰果。從他略微受傷

Pristine crystal sea / 清澈的海

的食指不難看出，他的刀一定很鋒利，同樣，他的頭腦也很敏銳。從他口中，我得知了 *Bulok Bulok* 這個名字背後的故事。

原來，這個島嶼及其周圍的海域曾經盛產章魚。當地人會抓來然後送往遙遠的市場出售。但那是在機動化時代之前，所以送到市場時，章魚已經全都腐爛了。因此大家都稱這個島為腐爛島。如今，島上的人們早都不做章魚生意了，但這個名字卻留了下來。臨別前，瑞可告訴我，他在腐爛島對面的島上有兩塊海濱土地出售。但因為比較偏遠，尤其腐爛島目前經濟狀態也不好，未來一段時間可能還是掛著賣不掉。

第三天，在我們抵達腐爛島之前，還停靠了許多庫里恩島的島嶼，比如帕斯雅克、坦邦、迪泰塔揚……當晚我們在船上過夜，我睡在上層甲板沒有床墊的硬地板上。到了第四天，我感覺我已經被太陽烤熟了，因為我從來不塗防晒乳。畢竟，我全身的皮膚可都經過了幾十年青藏高原地區最嚴酷的紫外線考驗。

All-purpose sports court / 多用途運動場　　　　Cockfight ring and homes / 鬥雞場與看台

我最後一次潛水是在艾希斯島。游回岸上時，我偶然發現腳邊有幾隻茂盛的海葵。我正猜想著會不會有小丑魚，果然，在海葵之間，四隻小尼莫輕快地游了出來，進進出出於海葵之間，彷彿在玩捉迷藏。這無疑讓我的一天變得更加美好，因為我找到了我的尼莫。

雖然只有短短四天，但當我走下那艘船時，感覺好像度日如年，離開住了好幾年的家。每天欣賞著日出和日落，長時的悠攔之際，宛如時間靜止。我們繼續前往艾爾尼多，在我朋友文斯培瑞茲位於直升機島的私人別墅中度過了兩日的悠閒時光。

那裡附近的石灰岩山丘成尖銳的脊椎狀矗立於一片純淨的瀉湖之中，大自然鬼斧神工的雕刻藝術令人驚嘆，讓我想起了巴塞隆納那座經歷了一百四十年仍在進化中的聖家堂。終於洗上一個真正的澡是我這次南海之旅最完美的結尾，圓夢之旅帶來的幸福回憶即使在漫長洶湧的時光中也永遠不會淡去。

Rico working on cashew / 瑞可在剝腰果　　　　　　　　Helicopter Island / 直升機島

在巴黎遇上騎兵

PARISIAN CALVARY ENCOUNTER

Paris – May 2, 2023

PARISIAN CALVARY ENCOUNTER

The rhythmic "clip clop" hoofbeat sound is clear and familiar. I used to hear it early morning some forty years ago while living in Kunming. Back then it was the sound of the horseshoes hitting the cement road outside my ground floor apartment, as the horse cart was leaving town after collecting night soil to use as fertilizer for the farms not far on the outskirt of town. Today, that outskirt is perhaps some twenty kilometers away.

But here it is, 21st Century downtown Paris just a couple blocks from the Bastille, and I am hearing the same sound, except that it is more paced and slower.

I open the door to my balcony and look down. Three horses with uniformed riders are just casually passing, with that rhythmic sound gradually fading away as they move further down the narrow road below me. I hastily take a few shots with my phone and send if off to my friendly host Federico. It is early Sunday morning and the synagogue across from me is all quiet.

"Would you like to visit the barracks from where these horses came? Five minutes' walk from my home." Federico texts back quickly from Spain. "Of course! Do they allow visits?" I asked. "Perfect, one of the guys in the picture is the colonel, I will ask him. The other is the general commanding

Synagogue across the house / 對街的猶太教堂　　　Flea market near Bastille / 巴士底監獄附近的跳蚤市場

the whole Garde Republicaine...," Federico writes back. That sounded perfect to quench my curiosity. After all, I hardly want to revisit the Eiffel Tower, the Louvre, Montmartre, the Lafayette or even the famous Paris flea market. Such an itinerary anyone could replicate.

Fifteen minutes later, my phone buzzes again. "How Man, Friday 10am at Celestins, Boulevard Henri IV n.22. Please ask at the poste de police for Mrs. Charlene G., thanks. She's the colonel's secretary, awaiting you tomorrow morning." Federico seems to have a Midas touch in setting things up. I was just in Sevilla for Easter, again as Federico's guest. Through him, I was inducted into the most exclusive men's club in the city during the busiest week of the year, Semana Santa, when days of religious processions wind through the narrow town streets.

In the past, I have stayed at some of his palacio homes in Italy, and now again in Paris. Federico is a Spinola, a

Bar/restaurant nearby / 附近的餐吧

member of the Genoan family from whom, some five hundred years ago, Columbus sought funding for his seafaring voyage to seek a new route to the Orient (and instead "discovered" America). That was perhaps one of the very first venture capital endeavors. Even the famous façade ruin of St. Paul's Church in Macao was drawn up by one of his family members who became a jesuit priest. Today my friend the Spinola continues to run a successful VC in managing his family office, with several famous global brands within his former portfolio. Perhaps it was because of that generational DNA that Federico found something worthy in my exploration work, and we have been fast friends ever since he visited my project sites in China.

True to Federico's word, the barracks of the Garde Republicaine, or Republican Guard, was indeed ten minutes' walk away and I was at its gate right at 10 AM. Two uniformed and armed female gendarmerie guards were at the entrance. Giving our contact's name of Charlene G. did the trick. A call was made and soon a tall and immaculately dressed woman walked up in stride and was in front of me.

Charlene led me into the huge tree-lined quadrangle courtyard of the barracks where riders were taking their stallions around the training ground in both directions of the track. She apologized for her deficiency in

Graphic Novel shop nearby / 附近的漫畫店

English while calling up a deputy, Christian, as our translator.

Charlene explained that there are three regiments of the Gendarmerie, a military police force guarding rural France and metro Paris. Among them are two infantry regiments and one regiment with three calvary squadrons that also take up both guard duties and ceremonial roles, including parade at the Champs-Elysees on Bastille Day. As a mounted force looks gallant to the public, especially to kids, they are most popular among the people in Paris. Their regular uniform is the same as the other regiments, but on ceremonial duties, they take on the most traditional and regal military costume bearing Paris's coat of arms, dating back to Napoleonic days. Details of protocol include that if the President is present, they must don white instead of blue pants.

We happened to visit on a day when an Italian military delegation was visiting and the Gendarmerie brass band was giving a reception performance. Those feathered silver helmets appeared shiny and most decorative on top of the dignified uniforms. The two drummers were particularly lively in delivering their act while the Italian officers stood on ceremony. We became the only spectators other than the Italians.

We were first led through a stable where the horses were kept as their homes, each to its own immaculately clean stall. Charlene explained that there are about 140 horses in the three squadrons, all issued from the finest Selle Francais breed. Each squadron has its own coat color of horses, the brass band and 1st squadron have chestnut horses (except the drum horses, which are white), the 2nd squadron bay horses and the 3rd brown bay, which is almost black.

At three years old, the horses are sent to a stud farm to be trained, then at four years old the best, mostly male, are chosen to serve in the squadron with each guard being assigned his or her own horse. The stallions are castrated on site at the barracks by one of five veterinary doctors with seven assistants at a small operating theater for such surgeries.

Next, we were shown the forge where the horses are shoed. Several men in leather work aprons were busy shoeing the horses, with furnaces burning in the back. Each horse's shoes were measured and custom-prepared to fit perfectly. Due to Paris' stringent pollution restrictions on coal-fired furnaces, nowadays the forgers had a little problem firing up the furnaces, which had been refitted with gas fire. Previously they could produce the horseshoes on site; now they buy various sizes, then modify and adapt them individually to each horse's foot.

I watched with amazement how the shoe-fitter craftsmen handled each horse by lifting one foot at a time, taking off the old shoe, eyeballing and measuring the foot, filing down the hoof's edges, then applying a new shoe with efficiency and grace. The horse would be calm and steady through the entire ordeal, as if being worked over by a babysitter changing diapers. Each horse was scheduled to change to new shoes every forty-five days, whether their old shoes were worn out or not. I felt Nike or Hermes should

Female riding guarde / 女騎兵
Stable holds for horses / 馬廠

enter this business, for show or for branding.

Finally, the renowned French designer/engineer Eiffel also made an unannounced appearance. We walked into a huge covered manege for the horses, used during rainy days or as an arena for shows to spectators, with grandstands on three sides of the "theater". I was told that the stunning roof structure was created by Gustave Eiffel.

Entering the calvary squadron is not as simple as being recruited into other armed services. Each new guard must be a skilled rider holding at least the French Galop 5 level, which can take years to achieve. Those successfully entering the force are not only given a horse but also staff quarters where they can live with their families.

Charlene is originally from Chalon-sur-Saone in Burgundy. She is now a mother of two young

Forging horse new shoe / 工人打造新馬蹄鐵

Trimming toe edges for new shoe /
磨平馬蹄邊緣以適應新鞋

Removing old shoe / 拆掉舊馬蹄

children, the younger one being born ten months ago. Her maternity duty has kept her off her horse now for over a year, and instead she has been assigned to desk duty. She hopes to be back on her saddle soon, within the next few months. Christian is also from outside of Paris in the southwest of France and is father to three children. Both of them live within the family quarters of the barracks.

Both Charlene and Christian have their own horses assigned, which they will keep for 16 to 18 years until the horses are retired. Upon retirement the horses are kept in stables outside of Paris for two years before being released for adoption. The guard then has first option to keep the horse for a nominal fee of one Euro but must promise to look after it with perfect care.

Having the best show horse can occasionally bring hurt. While each guard has his horse for the long term if, during a parade, the Colonel is keen on riding a specific horse, the rider must hand over his or her horse to him, meaning that that guard would not be able to participate in the parade. Such an incident can cost a few tears, but the rule must be abided by.

I look around and see that a great number of riders are women, and I ask Charlene the ratio. "Twenty years ago, when I first joined the Gendarmes, there were 4% women, but today our numbers are 57%," Charlene answered with obvious pride in her face at being among this elite troupe.

Charlene and Christian both like to spend their free time riding and also spend their holidays in the south of France when the horses are in pasture during July and August. Charlene loves to be in Issambres where she can easily take a ferry crossing the bay to Saint Tropez.

Charlene explaining Guarde duties / 夏琳正在解説

Two of the lesser known but very important duties of the Gendarmerie calvary guards are the monitoring of the precious grape harvest in Champagne to protect them from thieves, as well as monitoring the oyster beds just before the start of the harvest. Champagne lovers and oyster connoisseurs better be thankful!

I thank both Charlene and Christian profusely as we leave the barracks. Christian tears off his arm patch of the squadron as a memorabilia for me. Suddenly Charlene passes me a used horseshoe as a parting gift. "Remember, hang it up as in a U, not the other way round, or otherwise your luck will slip away," the beautiful guard cautioned me with a smart salute. I will certainly abide by her order, as this is the first time in my life I have been given an old shoe for good luck.

Charlene at stable hold / 馬廄前的夏琳

在巴黎遇上騎兵

外面「咔嚓，咔嚓」的馬蹄聲清晰地傳入我耳底，於我而言像是夢裡出現過的熟悉旋律。仔細回想，應該是四十年前我住在昆明的時候總是在清晨聽到的那種聲音。那是我一樓公寓外馬蹄鐵撞擊水泥路面發出的聲響，馬車在收集完前晚市內的糞便後出城，將其作為肥料運往不遠處的城郊農場。今天，那個城郊可能已經是在昆明市區二十公里開外了。

但在這裡，二十一世紀，離巴士底監獄僅有幾個街口的巴黎市中心，我又聽到了同樣的聲音，只是它更加有節奏且緩慢了些。

我打開陽台門向下望去，三個身穿制服的騎士正騎著馬徐徐而行地經過，他們沿著下方的窄路前進，韻律般的聲音逐漸遠去。我匆忙用手機拍了幾張照片，發送給我友善的好友房東費德里科。現在是週日的清晨，我對街的猶太教堂一片寧靜。

「你想不想去看看那些馬廄？從我家走路只要五分鐘。」費德里科回覆消息的速度相當迅速，即使他人在西班牙。「當然想！他們允許參觀嗎？」我問道。「好極了，照片中的一位是上校，我來問他看看。另一位是指揮整個共和國衛隊的將軍……」費德里科回覆說。這激起了我極大的興趣。畢竟，我可不想再去參觀艾菲爾鐵塔、羅浮宮、

蒙馬特高地、拉法葉或是著名的巴黎跳蚤市場，這樣的行程任何人都可以複製。

十五分鐘後，我的手機又響了。「嘿 HM，週五上午十點在第四區塞納河畔，亨利四世大道二十二號，請到警衛局去找夏琳女士，她是上校的祕書，明天早上會在那裡等你。」費德里科似乎有點點石成金的本領。我剛在塞維亞過完復活節，在那裡我也是住在他的房子。同樣，也是透過他的介紹，我在基督教傳統中一年裡最繁忙的一週，聖週，被引薦到了該市最神祕的男士俱樂部。彼時，持續了數天的節日遊行正把當地的街道堵得水泄不通。

我曾住過他在義大利的一些宮殿式住宅，如今在巴黎也是。費德里科是史賓諾拉家族的成員，大約五百年前，這個熱內亞家族曾經資助過哥倫布尋找通往東方的新航道，結果哥倫布意外發現了美洲新大陸，這也算是世界上最早的風險投資之一了。就連著名的澳門大三巴聖保羅教堂遺址，也是他家族一位出家當耶穌會傳教士成員製圖建成的。現在，我的朋友費德里科・史賓諾拉繼續成功地經營著他的家族企業，管理著幾個全球聞名的品牌。也許正是因為有著家族遺傳的「探險基因」，費德里科很欣賞和認同我在中國的探險工作，自從他參觀了我在中國的項目點以後，我們很快建立了親密的聯繫。

Garde Republicaine passing / 共和衛隊經過我窗下

Federico palacio home / 費德里科的宮殿式豪宅
Courtyard horse track / 騎馬跑道

費德里科說得沒錯，共和國衛隊的軍營確實離他的房子只有十分鐘的步行距離，我在上午十點準時到達了它的大門。兩名身穿制服、全副武裝的女憲兵把守在入口處。報上聯絡人夏琳女士的名字果然起上作用，守衛打了一通電話後不久，一位高挑、衣著考究的女士大步到我面前。

夏琳帶著我走進了一個連樹都排列得整整齊齊的四方形中庭，在那裡，騎士們正在訓練場的賽道上引導著他們的馬做往復跑練或踏步。夏琳謙虛地為自己英語不佳而道歉，隨即呼叫了她的副手克里斯丁來充當我們的翻譯。

夏琳解釋說，憲兵隊有三個團，是一支負責守衛法國鄉村和巴黎大都會的軍事警察部隊，其中包括兩個步兵團和一個由三個中隊組成的騎兵團，他們同時承擔警衛職責和官方儀式性角色，包括國慶日在香榭麗舍大道上遊行。騎兵部隊的形象在公眾，特別是孩子們眼裡是相當威武英勇的，因此騎兵們在巴黎群眾中非常受歡迎。他們的日常制服與其他軍團相同，但在履行儀式性職責時，他們會穿上最傳統、最華麗的軍服，並且配戴上可以追溯到拿破崙時代的巴黎市徽章。一些服飾規定的細節還包括，如果總統在場，他們必須穿白色而非藍色的長褲。

當天碰巧是義大利軍方代表團來訪的日子，憲兵隊的管弦樂隊正

在為他們進行接待表演。那些羽毛鑲嵌的銀色頭盔在尊嚴的制服上顯得閃閃發亮。兩位鼓手在表演中特別活躍，義大利軍官則特別嚴肅地站在一旁。現場的我們成了義大利人以外唯一的觀禮者。

接著，我們被帶到了一個馬廄，每匹馬都有自己的乾淨整潔的隔間。夏琳說，三個騎兵中隊約有一百四十匹馬，全都是最優良的賽拉法蘭西品種。每個中隊的馬都有其特定的毛色，管弦樂隊和第一中隊是栗色的，鼓手的馬比較特別，牠們是白色的，第二中隊是紅褐色的，第三中隊則是接近黑色的紅褐色。

馬兒們滿三歲時就要被送往馬場接受訓練，四歲時馬場會選出最優秀的馬兒去騎兵中隊服役，通常

Brass band honoring Italian officers / 歡迎義大利軍官的管樂隊

情況下被選中的都是公馬。每位衛兵都會被分配到獨屬於自己的馬兒。軍營中有一個專門為閹割手術而設的小型手術室，公馬們在服役前都得在這兒走一遭。

打鐵鋪是給馬兒裝蹄鐵的地方。幾位身穿皮質工作圍裙的匠人忙著給馬兒釘上鐵蹄，爐火在後方熊熊燃燒。每匹馬的鐵鞋都經過嚴密測量，定制得天衣無縫。由於巴黎對燃煤爐的汙染限制嚴苛，鍛造師傅們必須將熔爐改裝成燒瓦斯。這就加大了鐵蹄製作的難度，在此之前，他們可以現場製作馬蹄鐵，而現在，他們只能先購買各種尺寸的鐵鞋，再根據馬兒們的腳碼逐一調整。

這些工匠們爐火純青的手藝讓我看了嘖嘖稱奇。一次舉起一隻蹄子，取下舊鐵鞋，目測量度蹄子，銼平蹄緣，然後高效地裝上新鐵鞋，甚至這個過程還有點行雲流水的優雅。馬兒在整個過程中非常淡定，彷彿是一個新生兒正在被一個溫柔的保姆伺候著換尿布。規定是每匹馬每四十五天必須更換新鐵鞋，不論舊鐵鞋是否磨損。我覺得耐吉或愛瑪仕應該來做這一行，對做噱頭、品牌推廣肯定很有效。

行至一處馬場時，我不禁被它那堪稱巧奪天工般的穹頂所震撼。問了才知，這是聲名顯赫的巴黎鐵塔法國設計師兼工程師艾菲爾的作品。這個馬場可以用作雨天時馬匹訓練的場地，也經常作為面向觀眾的競技場，三面設有看台，頗像一座「劇院」。

加入騎兵中隊要比進入其他軍事單位難得多。每位新兵都必須擁有相當熟練的騎術，量化來說，至少持有法國賽馬會五級資格證書，而這可需要花費多年時間才能達成，所以成功加入部隊的人待遇也相對不錯，不僅會被分配到一匹專屬馬，還有可以與家

HM with tall horse / HM 與高大的駿馬

人一起居住的員工宿舍。

夏琳出身於勃艮地索恩河畔沙隆鎮，現在已經是兩個小孩的母親了，小的那個剛出生十個月。因為要照顧小孩，她不得已被調到文職，她說她很渴望能重回馬鞍之上，最好幾個月之內就能實現，看來，她正為此努力。克里斯丁也不是巴黎本地人，他來自法國西南部的巴黎郊外，是三個孩子的父親。他們倆人都住在營區裡的員工宿舍。

夏琳和克里斯丁都有屬於自己的馬，他們陪伴馬兒十六至十八載，直至馬兒退役。退役後，這些馬兒會在巴黎郊外的馬廄中安養兩年，然後開放供人領養。騎兵們有權以象徵性的一歐元進行優先收養，但必須承諾要盡心盡力地照顧牠們。

有時如果馬兒過於出色，反倒會導致主人的傷悲。在遊行期間，若上校相中了某匹馬，騎士必須無條件讓出，這意味著該騎兵將無緣參加遊行。這樣的事情雖然很令人遺憾，但軍規不容違背。

我環顧四周，發現許多騎手是女性，便詢問夏琳這其中的性別比例。她自豪地答道：「二十年前我剛剛加入憲兵隊時，女性只占百分之四，但今天我們的比例已達百分之五十七。」她的臉上寫滿了作為這支精英部隊女性一員的驕傲。

休假時，夏琳和克里斯丁還是喜歡騎馬消遣。每年七八月分，馬匹在法國南部牧場放牧時，他們會選擇在那裡度假。夏琳特別鍾愛伊桑布雷村，從那邊她可以乘渡輪穿越海灣，輕鬆抵達聖特羅佩。

值得一提的是，騎兵隊有個不為人知卻至關重要的職責：防盜。每當收穫季節來臨，他們都要打起精神守護用來做精品香檳的名貴葡萄和養殖場裡的牡蠣，以免賊手侵擾。香檳愛好者和牡蠣鑑賞家們應該對此心存感激啊！

我們離開軍營時，對夏琳和克里斯丁表達了深深的謝意。克里斯丁撕下他的中隊臂章，作為給我的紀念品。夏琳給了我一個用過的馬蹄鐵作為告別禮物。「記住，正 U 型才是對的配掛方式，不要倒轉，否則會倒霉的。」這位美麗的騎兵隊員語氣嚴肅地「警告」我，順帶敬了一個乾淨利落的禮。我肯定會遵從她的吩咐，畢竟這是我生平第一次收到「舊鞋」這種禮物。要知道，在中華文化語境裡，舊鞋的象徵意義與「祝福」可是南轅北轍呀。

Manege with Eiffel designed roof / 馬兒們在艾菲爾建造的屋頂下練習

Emblem of the squadron / 中隊臂章

神
祕
的
不
丹
東
部

BHUTAN EAST

Paro, Bhutan – May 16, 2023

BHUTAN EAST
A royal reception in Kingdom of the Thunder Dragon

The roads are rough and unpaved, not unlike my early exploration of Tibet some forty years ago. But it is understandable, as we are at the eastern end of Bhutan on the way to some of the most remote communities of this Himalayan kingdom. However, soon this bad road will be history, as the tar-topping machine can be seen paving sections of this last stretch of the road. The pace of change is slow but steady, like much else in this Druk kingdom, or the Land of the Dragon.

The Landcruiser I am in takes the turns and switch backs of the road with ease, kicking up a trail of dust in its wake. Behind the wheel are a pair of steady hands. These are no ordinary hands, but those of Ashi Kesang. I would love to be behind the wheel myself, but it is not to be. She loves driving and has taken on such roads since the age of thirteen, when she was given the keys by her mother for the first time and told to drive east.

Downshifting without a thought as we approached a curve, she pulls the car out of the corner while accelerating with ease. I can feel her full confidence in maneuvering this man-sized SUV through the most difficult mountain roads. My sexist notions of "man-sized car" and "woman driver" must not slip from my lips. Instead, Ashi, meaning princess, would occasionally snap : "Woman driver!"

when she was slowed down by some lately liberated female driver while driving through the capital town of Thimphu. One small modifier – Ashi often drives in her kira, the traditional costume of a long skirt stretching far down beyond her knees to her ankles.

We are heading into Merak, a small community at the end of the road. As usual, I am curious about the furthest points of each country, call them frontier regions or fringe areas, at worst "disputed" area.

Ashi's quiet voice and gentle demeanor can be a camouflage for her and delusionary to others. But her mind is strong like the metal steel chains of the iron bridges built by Thangtong Gyalpo, the legendary 14th century master builder and sage of Tibet. At one point we stopped at Tachog Gomba, a monastery near the border of Tashigang and Yangtse, the two eastern Dzongs, or districts, and my focus on this trip. The small monastery is near a former site of one such bridge and protects relics in the form of huge iron chains encased behind glass on display.

Perhaps a note on Thangtong Gyalpo is appropriate here. A Da Vinci of the plateau, a renaissance man of Tibet, he came to Bhutan seven hundred years ago and successfully constructed ten iron suspension bridges as models for his later engineering feats throughout Tibet. In order to

Paro Dzong & palace / 帕羅城堡與宮殿
Rainbow on Tashigang Dzong / 宗城堡的彩虹

Relic bridge chains / 古橋的鐵鍊

raise funds for building such bridges, he founded Tibetan opera with a traveling troupe of six sisters to raise money. On top of that he was a master architect with many important temples built under his watch. He is also revered as the medicinal deity for his knowledge of traditional healing methods. During the pandemic, his statues flooded the market in Lhasa. My connection to this deity is through a statue of him that Ashi's grandmother had chosen as a gift for me.

Ashi has inherited her grandmother's strong mind and valor in execution for preserving the traditional cultural and religious heritage of the kingdom. No sophisticated packaging and fancy words are needed - despite her western education, her track record speaks louder than words. We are proud to share the same modus operandi.

Her grandmother is none other than the Royal Grandmother Ashi Kesang Choden Wangchuck. The Ashi behind the wheel of my car, by chance or by design, carries exactly the same name as Her Majesty, now 94 years of age, who is very much my patron whenever I visit Bhutan. The benefits include, not least, that my humble body is allowed to take up temporary refuge inside some of the off-site palaces at Her Majesty's gracious discretion.

While staying at the Paro Palace, I managed to host our CERS directors on our board retreat for tea one afternoon. Her Majesty arranged for a morning breakfast at the Namseyling Palace for directors on the day of their arrival. The next day a sumptuous lunch was prepared at her Royal Palace after she gave a wonderful audience to all the directors present, and showered everyone with royal gifts. As before, I was given bottles of health supplement pills, a concentrate concoction made from Her Majesty's royal supply of Cordyceps, and two wooden crates of "Royal Jelly", or jam, made from fruit grown in her garden. I felt honored as well as humbled to be offered a red khata ceremonial scarf. Usually, a white one would be given as blessings and courtesy.

Her Majesty on this trip also provided me the use of a palace car, though with the flag covered, and an experienced driver during the entire two-weeks stay of my time in the kingdom. Now, in the east, that is our escort vehicle, which has taken two full days drive to get here. For some reason, with two cars fielded, I feel more safe and special sitting in a car driven by Ashi the princess.

Our trip out east is to fill my desire to have a brief look at Bhutan away from the tourist routes, and hopefully to

Remains of iron bridge on display / 展示櫃中的鐵橋殘骸

Temple near iron bridge / 鐵橋附近的寺廟

develop some worthy projects in the future among the remotest corners of the kingdom. I always remind myself, a life-long geographer, that Bhutan is larger than Taiwan or Belgium, yet with a population of 1/30th and 1/15th that of the other two respectively.

As labor or man power is obviously not its best asset, the kingdom has gone for brain prowess and happiness power. Bhutan developed what is now known the world over as its GNH, Gross National Happiness index, as opposed to the rest of the world's GDP index. Measuring each country's development based on a scale of per capita income by averaging the numbers seems delusionary and incomplete, if not archaic, as it takes no account of the social safety net nor infrastructure investment. Let alone distribution of proceeds are highly uneven. Neither can economists account for where each country's GDP growth has gone. Toward a broad per capita distribution? Or totally lop-sided, toward a few individuals' top-end pockets. We perhaps need more socially equitable economists in this world.

What Bhutan has achieved with a tiny population, despite being a land-locked country sandwiched delicately between the two rising powerhouses of India and China, has been phenomenal and most worthy of respect. The next phase of growth, however, may be more challenging. The kingdom faces an exodus of brains and educated people to Australia after the pandemic, as opportunities overseas are becoming an attraction for the younger set.

CERS is a tiny entity with limited resources. So we have always focused on small and remote communities where we feel our small help can produce some substantial impact, as opposed to the big data and impact by scale so popular in the digital world today. Our partner communities are often off the map and neglected. Thus, my request to have a look at two small communities in eastern Bhutan, Merak and Sakteng, both within the region of Tashigang. We went also up northeast to briefly cover the region of Yangtse, bordering Tibet and India.

My flight from Thimphu the capital to Tashigang in the east in a brand new twin turboprop ATR 42 took 45 minutes. Landing on a strip high up on a ridge was exciting. The drive into town took around twenty minutes and we stopped to visit Sherubtse College, the first university in Bhutan. Set up in 1968, it is now under the administration of the Royal University of Bhutan in Thimphu. I find it amazing that Bhutan would set up its first university in a faraway Dzongkhag in order to lift the poorest part of the kingdom upward; very strategic and forward thinking indeed.

Two of the deans Dendup Tshering and Paljor Galay, of the school of Research and student affairs respectively walked me through campus, observing student in class or in small groups in the well-manicured green lawn. I made a visit to the library, peeked into classrooms and dormitories, then the canteen and kitchen, and ended by taking a simple lunch at the university café. Students did not have school uniforms but were all wearing traditional national costume.

Lunch at Royal Grandmother palace /
皇太后宮殿內的午餐
Breakfast at Namseyling Palace / 舊皇宮早餐

The deans told me that the university used to have many Indian professors helping in teaching and development of curriculum, but now it is totally independent and run by Bhutanese. They also have a few foreign professors including two from the U.S. I hope in time, I can make a connection for the university with two other schools I am involved with, University of Hong Kong and Westlake University in Hangzhou China.

After lunch, we checked into a posh traditional hotel. I was delighted that I was assigned the huge room with reception chamber usually reserved for the King when he visited the eastern region. The refrigerator was stocked with some wonderful beverages. The chamber was highly decorated and overlooked the Dzong castle below at a distance. At night, the monumental edifice on the cliff side was lit up nicely, showing its full majesty.

The following day we visited Merak and stayed the night at a spartan yet clean home-stay house. The colorfully dressed women wore black yak caps that were unique, with five strings curling out like legs from the rim. Functionally these serve to drain rainwater and prevent it dripping into their faces. While being led through the village and its immediate surrounding, we were entertained with multiple stories as the village chief pointed to every shape of rock along the path to illustrate legends, deities, or devils, with all seriousness. I was also able to collect a traditional bow with arrows, with the bow collapsible into two parts for easy transport. A double-tube bamboo flute and weaved rug also are now within our collection of ethnic objects.

In the evening, six ladies dressed in their best and most colorful costumes showed up to offer us

Students of the college / 大學的學生們

songs and ceremonial *ara*, a local fermented liquor. At each interval of a song, a bowl of this strong liquor would be poured into my mouth. I was force fed more or less, as at the same time, several hands would be onto various parts of my body - my arm, my waist, my thigh, and even my ears - pinching so hard that I would open my mouth to cry out "Ouch!" at which point the drink would be successfully administered. These three rounds of drink, I suppose, are meant to insure that the special guest will always remember his gracious hosts.

The next day we visited Sakteng, another small community, through even worse roads. Later that day, we drove up to Tashi Yangtse, the northeastern Dzong of Bhutan. As with all Dzong forts, it housed the monastic body and the government offices. I always admired the castle-like architecture and design of these buildings, let alone the effort of building them at the most precarious locations.

At two of the monasteries, we were shown the ancient relics and Thangka scroll paintings. There were two *tashigomang*, meter-tall, pagoda-shaped, portable religious ornaments that have become extremely rare in Bhutan and obsolete throughout Tibet. With Ashi Kesang, and with Sonam as our

Preparing liquor for guests / 當地人為客人準備的特色酒
Singing to guest / 當地人熱情地為客人獻唱
Weaver of Merak / 梅拉克的編織工

attending monk, it was decided that these two objects require immediate restoration as they were dilapidated and falling apart. It was arranged on site that soon they would be sent to the Restoration Center in Thimphu for work.

It is said that villagers of both Bhutan near Merak and Sakteng and those from Tawang of India, cross the border regularly either for trading or as pilgrims to sacred sites on both sides of the border. Tawang, being the birth place of the romantic and poetic 6th Dalai Lama, is considered very holy. However, during the pandemic, all cross-border traffic was suspended, and it has yet to reopen for pilgrims.

After four short days in the east, we began our arduous two-day drive back to Thimphu. We spent a night in Bumthang in a Swiss-built lodge and arrived in the capital the following day just in time for dinner. My thirst for seeing the east is quenched. But to be deserving of the graciousness bestowed on me by the Royal Grandmother, as well as by the ladies who serenaded me with toasts, would not be as easy. Perhaps building a connection to the university would be a first step in the right direction.

Stupa in temple / 寺廟裡的佛塔

神祕的不丹東部

來自雷龍之國皇室般的接待

道路坎坷且未鋪砌，頗似四十年前我初探西藏之時的景象。然而這也在情理之中，畢竟我們正位於不丹東端，在去往這喜馬拉雅王國中一些最偏遠地區的路上。不過，當我看到一些瀝青鋪設機的工作已經接近尾聲時，我知道，這條糟糕的道路即將成為歷史。進步的步調緩慢而又堅定，正如這個「雷龍之國」（宗喀語中的不丹國名），或稱「龍之國」中的萬事萬物。

我乘坐的豐田陸地巡洋艦越野車輕鬆應對著連綿迴轉的道路，車後留下一串串揚塵。方向盤上是一雙穩健的手──這並非尋常之手，而是不丹公主 Ashi Kesang 的手。我是想親自駕駛的，但拗不過她執意要當司機。她說她很喜歡開車，從十三歲第一次被母親給予鑰匙起，她就在這凹凸不平的道路上行車了。她的母親只告訴她，握住方向盤後，一路向東行。

車行駛近彎道時，她俐落地減檔，然後再輕鬆地加速過彎。目睹這一切的我能清楚地感受到她的自信滿滿，即使是面對在崎嶇的山路上駕馭這輛大塊頭 SUV 這樣的「難題」。所以我默默地讓「只有男人才能駕馭的大尺寸車」和「女司機」等刻板印象名詞往肚裡吞。反倒是 Ashi 公主偶爾會吐槽，比如當我們在首都延布的路上被女司機拖慢時，她會很可愛地抱怨：「一看就是女司機啊！」Ashi 常常穿著她們傳統的筒裙服

Ashi Kesang at the wheel / 駕駛席的 Ashi Kesang

Tashigang / 俯瞰視角下的塔希岡

飾 *Kira* 開車，*Kira* 是一種做工精美的長裙，長度從膝蓋一直垂到腳踝。

現在，我們正朝著道路盡頭的一個小村落梅拉克前進。像往常一樣，我對每個國家最偏遠的地帶滿懷好奇，一般這樣的地區都被叫做邊疆或者邊緣地帶，更甚有時還稱爭議點。

請不要因為 *Ashi Kesang* 有著溫柔的聲線和優雅的舉止就誤認為她是個傳統意義上的柔弱女子，她的內心可是像十四世紀西藏傳奇建築大師湯東傑布建造的鐵橋上的鋼鍊一樣堅強。在旅途中，我們曾在達邱寺停留，這座寺廟坐落在塔希岡村和央奇兩個東部行政區的交界處，也是我們此行的重點。達邱寺靠近我提到過的湯東傑布建造的鐵橋遺址，寺廟的玻璃櫃中還保存著巨大的鐵鍊遺跡。

在此處提及湯東傑布可不是毫無緣由的。他是高原上的達文西，是西藏文化和藝術精華的代表。

Gifts to CERS directors / 送給董事們的禮物

七百年前，他來到不丹，為這裡的人們建立了十座鐵索橋，也為他之後在西藏地區的工程壯舉打下了經驗基礎。為了籌集建造鐵橋的資金，他帶著六個比丘尼組建了一個西藏歌劇團，進行巡迴演出募捐。除了橋的建築，當地很多具有重要意義的寺廟也在這位傑出的建築大師的監督下建成。甚至在醫學方面，湯東傑布也頗有建樹。他因掌握著藏族傳統治療術方面的精深知識而被尊稱為醫藥之神。在新冠疫情期間，西藏的大街小巷都供奉著他的雕像。*Ashi* 的祖母皇太后就曾送我一尊他的雕像，那算是我與這位聖人結緣的開始。

Ashi 繼承了她祖母強大的意志力和執行力，在保存不丹王國的傳統文化與宗教遺產方面不遺餘力。她不需要華麗的包裝和粉飾的詞藻，西方的高等教育背景也算不上她的加分項，她在文化保育方面的成就已經勝過一切言語。我們都很自豪於能在工作和處世之道方面有很多共識。

Ashi 的祖母正是不丹王室的皇太后阿希‧格桑‧卻旺楚克，不知是偶然還是有意為之，駕駛我車子的 *Ashi* 與現年九十四歲、每當我訪問不丹時總是充當我的靠山的皇太后陛下的名字一模一樣。皇太后的庇護給我帶來了許多好處，最令我受寵若驚的是，我這「平民」的身軀被獲准可以暫居在皇室的一些行宮內。

某個在帕羅宮停留的下午，我設法招待我們中國探險學會的董事們來喝下午茶。非常讓我感動和感謝的是，董事們抵達的當天早晨，皇太后就幫我安排了大家在皇家南謝林宮享用早餐。隔天，陛下又在她的皇宮內準備了豐盛的午餐，在給予所有在場董事們極佳的接見後，慷慨地為每人送上了皇家禮物。我也收到了一份與往常一樣的禮物，數瓶保健補充藥丸，這是從陛下的皇家冬蟲夏草貯藏中提煉出來的。禮物中還有兩個裝滿「皇家蜂王漿」的木箱，我也願意稱之為皇家果醬，那是由她自家花園中種植的果實製成。當被贈與一條紅色哈達時，我感到無比榮幸和謙卑。因為通常作為祝福和禮貌，白色的哈達就已足夠。

皇太后還提供了宮廷專用轎車供我在此行使用，為了低調行事，車旗被遮蓋，同時在我停留不丹王國的整整兩週期間，都一直有一位經驗豐富的司機隨行。現在，在我們開了兩整天才到達的不丹東部，那輛被派來的宮廷車更像是我乘坐的這輛車的隨行護衛。不知何故，即使另一輛車有專業的司機，我卻覺得坐在由 Ashi 駕駛的車內更安全也更榮幸。

我們此行一路向東，是為了滿足我想要拋開既定的旅遊人士路線，簡略地瞥見不丹真實面貌的願望。我非常希望未來能在不丹王國最偏遠的角落發展一些有價值的項目。當了快一輩子的「地理學者」，我總是喜歡做一些具象化的比較，比如不丹的國土面積比台灣和比利時大，然而人口分別只有它們的三十分之一和十五分之一。

人口勞動力顯然不是不丹王國的優勢所在，所以這個國家轉而追求智慧實力和幸福指數。不丹制定了如今全世界皆知的國民幸福總值（GNH）指數，與世界上絕大多數國家追求的國內生產總值（GDP）指數完全背道而馳。根據人均收入的平均數來衡量每個國家的發展程度在我看來是失真的，因分配所得是不平均的。既不完整，又過時。因為它甚至沒有考慮到社會安全網絡和基礎設施投資。

First university of Bhutan / 不丹的第一所大學
Rare books at library / 圖書館中的珍奇圖書

我想，經濟學家也無法解釋每個國家的 GDP 增長到底去向何處。是朝著廣泛地人均分配方向發展？還是完全偏向少數階層人的口袋？或許這個世界需要更多注重社會公平的經濟學家。

不丹雖然是閉關鎖國的內陸國家，微妙地夾在中國和印度兩個崛起的大國之間，但是它以微小的人口所取得的成就是驚人且十分令人敬佩的。不過，它下一階段的成長可能會更具挑戰性。不丹王國在疫情後面臨著嚴峻的人才流失，尤其是面向澳大利亞的外流。海外的發展機會正像不可抗拒的漩渦一樣吸引著不丹王國的年輕一代出走。

中國探險學會是一個資源有限的小單位，因此，我們一直專注於小型和偏遠的地區，對比現今數字世界流行的大數據和規模衝擊，我更傾向於在那些特定的小地方讓我們的幫助產生一些實質性的影響。也因此，我們的很多項目點在如今各個發達的線上地圖上都找不到。所以，這次我貫徹原則，要求參觀不丹東部的兩個小社區——梅拉克（Merak）和薩克滕（Sakteng），兩者都位於塔希岡（Tashigang）區域內。我們還向東北部前進，簡要探訪了與西藏和印度接壤的央奇地區。

從首都廷布到東部的塔希岡，我飛行了四十五分鐘，乘坐的是全新的雙渦槳 ATR 42 飛機。記憶猶新的是降落在山脊上的跑道很是

刺激。從機場開車進城大約需要二十分鐘，中途我們停下來參觀了成立於一九六八年的不丹境內第一所大學，夏魯伯希學院（*Sherubtse College*），它現在由首都廷布的不丹皇家大學管理。我認為，不丹在遙遠的宗喀區設立其第一所大學，以謀求改善王國最貧窮的部分發展水平的舉動，實在是非常具有戰略性和前瞻性的。

夏魯伯希學院研究與學生事務學院的兩位院長登杜·慈仁（*Dendup Tshering*）和帕佐·加雷（*Paljor Galay*）陪我參觀了校園。路過修剪整齊的綠色草坪時，我欣慰地看到學生們正認真地聽課或分小組討論。我還參觀了圖書館，偷瞄了幾眼教室和宿舍、餐廳和廚房，最後在大學咖啡廳簡單地用過午餐。學生們沒有統一的校服，但都穿著傳統的國家民族服裝。

院長們告訴我，這所大學過去曾有許多印度教授幫忙授課和進行課程研發，但現在已完全獨立地由不丹人經營。他們也有幾位外國教授，其中有兩位來自美國。聽及此，我非常希望能夠為這所大學與另外兩所跟我有合作的學校建立聯繫，也就是香港大學和中國杭州的西湖大學。

Audience chamber at Tashigang /
塔希岡的接待室

Tashigang Dzong in evening / 塔希岡城堡夜景

Royal Room / 皇室寢殿

午餐後，我們入住了一家豪華的不丹傳統酒店。我很高興自己被安排到了一間有接待室，通常保留給國王訪問東部地區時使用的大房間。房間裝飾華麗，冰箱裡貼心地儲備了一些我喜歡的飲品，從窗戶的視角還可以遠眺到下方的宗堡。夜幕降臨時，懸崖邊的那座堡壘燈火通明，氣勢莊嚴。

翌日，我們探訪了梅拉克（Merak）地區，並在一間簡樸但乾淨整潔的旅舍過夜。當地婦女們身著五彩繽紛的服裝，頭戴獨特的黑色犛牛毛帽，帽沿上卷出的五條線好像人類伸展出的肢體。這種帽子的功能實際上是用來引導雨水流下，防止其滴落到臉上。村長一邊認真地講解，一邊帶我們穿越整個村莊。他說沿途每一塊形狀各異的石頭都承載著一段傳說，或關於神祇，或關於魔鬼。我還收集到了一套傳統的弓和箭，弓可以分成兩部分折疊起來，便於攜帶，我順便還將一支雙管竹笛和一張編織的地毯加入了我們的民族物品收藏庫。

傍晚，六位盛裝打扮的女士為我們獻上了歌曲和當地一種叫 Ara 的特色發酵烈酒。每當歌曲間隔，便有一碗濃酒倒入我的口中。我多少算是被灌酒，因為同時有好幾隻手按住我的全身各處——手臂、腰部、大腿，甚至他們還會捏我的耳朵，以至於我張口大叫「哎喲！」，每當這時，我就被灌酒成功了。酒過三巡，我漸漸反應過來，這麼特殊的勸酒方式可能是為了讓貴賓們永遠記得他們慷慨熱情的主人吧！

隔天，我們參訪了另一個小村落薩克滕，通向那裡的道路更為崎嶇。那天晚些時候，我們駛向塔希揚策，不丹東北部的宗堡。如同所有宗堡一樣，它既是僧侶的修行之地，也是政府的辦公地點。我總是沉醉於這些建築的風格和精妙的設計，也實在敬佩在如

Chorten Kora in Tashi Yangtze / 塔西央奇的科拉佛塔

此險峻的地點建造它們所付出的巨大努力。

在兩座寺院中，我們見到了古老的文物和唐卡卷軸畫。我們還見到了兩座多福門，這種約一米高的寶塔形狀、便於攜帶的宗教飾物在不丹已經變得極為稀有，在整個西藏更是絕跡。在跟 Ashi 和陪同我們的僧侶索南共同商議後，公主決定立即修復這兩個殘破不堪、破碎散落的多福門，於是馬上安排人手將它們送往位於廷布的修復中心進行維修工作。

據說，不丹境內靠近梅拉克和薩克滕的村民們與印度達旺的居民會經常跨越邊境進行貿易，也會有人到對方國家的朝聖地去朝聖。達旺是著名的「浪漫詩人」第六代達賴喇嘛倉央嘉措的出生地，一直以來都被視為神聖之地。然而在疫情期間，所有的跨境交通都被暫停了，朝聖者的邊境通道至今尚未重新開放。

在東部短暫停留了四天後，接下來就是同樣艱難的回廷布的兩日車程。中途我們在不丹布姆塘的一家瑞士式旅舍過了夜，隔天到回首都時恰好趕上晚餐。至此，我對初步了解不丹東部的願望已得到滿足。但是，要避免辜負皇太后陛下的恩惠，以及那些用美酒和歌聲款待我的女士們的好意，可不是那麼簡單的事情。我想，或許，幫助不丹的大學建立對外合作關係會是向正確方向邁進的第一步。

Tashigang Dzong fortress / 塔希冈的古堡
Fortress courtyard / 古堡中的庭院

再訪一觸即發的西藏邊界

TO TIBET FLASHPOINT BORDER ONCE MORE

Le Tibet – June 5, 2023

TO TIBET FLASHPOINT BORDER ONCE MORE

Lebugou is a gorge of the Namka River that flows from Tsona County in southern Tibet into India-controlled Tawang district. Nearby are our small villages on the China-controlled side of a disputed border, north of the controversial McMahon line. These are all Menpa villages, significant in that they have the same historical, cultural and religious heritage as those of the same ethnic people living south of the line. Le Village where I am is the one closest to the border.

The powerful 5th Dalai Lama set up the Tawang region as one of the tribute states from which Lhasa could collect tariff and as supplicant to the Tibetan court in the 1600s. The entire region was then called Menyu, as opposed to the other two "yu's" to the east, Zayu and Lhoyu. Inhabitants here were mainly Menpa, with some Lhopa and Tibetans. It was with such territorial context that the poetic and romantic 6th Dalai, born in Tawang, became reincarnation of the Great 5th.

The two areas of Merak and Sakteng within Trashigang Dzong, formerly part of Tawang, were previously considered undefined and disputed territories between China and Bhutan but were generously "given" to Bhutan by India, since India controlled the region upon exit of the former British colonial government. Now it is a de facto part of Bhutan. However, in 2020 just as Bhutan started to set up the Sakteng Wildlife Sanctuary, China made an unsettling objection, citing the area as still under dispute.

I had the great good fortune to visit the Bhutan side barely a month or so ago. Now I am in the Tibetan Autonomous Region just on the other side of the border near where three countries meet in apparent peace, hopefully with no storm looming. Recently, there have even been rumors circulating that China and Bhutan, after over twenty rounds of discussion and negotiations, have accepted that Merak and Sakteng are within Bhutan's national border, just as the maps are drawn today. This is said to be in return for Bhutan accepting to forego some hundreds of square kilometers of disputed territories to the north, somewhat near the village of Le where I am now. How an explorer is always caught up in frontier disputed areas, on both sides of the border, is anyone's guess.

Through diplomatic exchanges and negotiations, China has over the last few decades settled many territorial disputes with neighboring countries, usually conceding land for peace. Somehow with small countries, China could afford to be generous, amicable, and give grace; whereas with big power players, it would become far more forceful and assertive. Just as issues over the South China Sea and Taiwan are flaring up as international geopolitical contests, discussion between the two most populous countries in the world continue to evade resolution. Minor border skirmishes, if not

South of the Himalayas / 喜瑪拉雅山南
Deep gorge of Lebugou / 勒布溝的深深峽谷

contained with cool heads, may escalate to become real or rhetorical wars between these two giant neighbors. My last visit to Tsona in 1987 was during such a tense moment when troops were deployed on both sides of the China-India border.

We have just dropped down from the stratospheric altitude of over 5000 meters above sea level to forest under 3000 meters on the south slopes of the Himalayas here at the villages of Mamaxiang and Le, or Lexiang Village. It is less than 50 km to Sakteng and 40 km to Tashi Yangtse as a crow flies, or 30 km to Tawang. My border permit allows my team to visit places up to the frontiers and I wanted to pay respect at a small temple where Guru Rinpoche, founder of the Nyingma Sect of Tibetan Buddhism, had spent time in meditation, supposedly leaving an old hat behind. When Guru Rinpoche came from India to Tibet, he supposedly subdued the local evil witch, and her fossilized bones are now visible as a rock there. There are many other relic remains of Guru Rinpoche, illustrated by sign boards around the site.

Village of Mamaxiang / 瑪瑪鄉　　　　　　Le Village closest to border / 最接近邊界的勒村

The hike up to the tiny Xinmuja shrine temple takes about half an hour. I mixed in with a few small groups of Tibetan pilgrims from Lhasa, but we were careful to avoid the troop of wild monkeys, which tend to harass visitors since some tourists have the bad habit of feeding or teasing them. One lone senior monk, Awang Oser, acts as caretaker of the place. He is not too eager to be photographed, nor to entertain guests. Tsomo, my research assistant, is Tibetan and manages to charm him to unlock the shrine for our quick visit. A beautiful waterfall showers down next to the premises creating a perpetual rainbow as the sun shines its light over the sparkle of water.

We run into Quzhoung (43) who is taking her turn in sweeping the stone path towards and around the temple. Such rotation of volunteer work is done by members of Le Village. Together with husband Dorboji (47) she has three children. The eldest son has graduated from university and is working in a neighboring village as secretary, while the younger one is still in third year university. The adopted daughter is also a university grad, so the parents must feel very proud and contented. Such changes in a formerly deprived frontier region are not unique and are becoming more common place. Many Menpa here are involved in a community tea growing and processing

Xinmuja Shrine / 錫如努迦神殿   Inside small shrine / 神殿內部

cooperative. Its prime quality tea is in limited supply but sold throughout Tibet.

Today Le has 32 households with over 70 adults in the families. Since 2017, the government has executed a new policy to build houses and create opportunities for minimum prosperity among 628 marginal villages along Tibet's national border. Le is one such village community that benefited from the policy's implementation.

The policy focuses on providing clean water, electricity, road access, education in science and humanities, healthcare and hygiene improvements. For the newly constructed houses, the government invests 70% whereas the locals must put in 30%. They then rebuild on former village sites with villa-like family homes. Some of the smaller and remote families are also relocated into the new village. It is hoped that the sacred border temple will bring in pilgrim and tourist income for the villagers.

In the past, there was sporadic border trading among Menpa on both sides of the border, as well as limited numbers of pilgrims from Tawang region. Since the pandemic, however, such activities have come to a halt and have not been restored. Perhaps joint development of some conflict areas as special buffer zones can be an arbitrated solution for the future. After all, these neighbors are not going away, so they might as well learn to live with each other, despite historical, cultural, religious or political similarities or differences.

In between visits to the border region, we camped for two nights by the Namka Chu River cascading

Rainbow waterfall / 彩虹瀑布

through the gorges, site of the field headquarters of General Zhang Guohua when he launched the major battle between India and China in 1962. In China, this is known as the Battle of Kegyenam, which lasted for nine days from October 15 to 24.

The PLA pushed through to the plain of Tawang in a decisive advance and annihilated the Indian forward army, before unilaterally calling a cease fire and retreating back to the former line of control. Apparently, their point was made on the battlefield. Since then, for some sixty years, the relationship of the two countries has been cool and never quite returned to the honeymoon years of the 1950s. Today, there is a small exhibit museum across the river from where we stayed, with a display and mock-up of camps illustrating the era of that battle.

The exchange of accusations never ended, with each country holding its own opinion of cause, effect and interpretation of the conflict. Perhaps one Western journalist turned scholar held a more neutral stance, though

Display of border terrain / 邊界地區模型展示
Local tourists at exhibit site / 展覽現場的當地遊客
Map of 1962 battle on display / 展館中 1962 年的戰役圖

some may call his account revisionist. Neville Maxwell, an Australian and correspondent in India for the London Times at the time of the conflict, switched his angle after getting his hands on the Indian Army's internal secret papers, the Henderson-Brooks Report, and wrote the seminal book "India's China War". For decades now, he has been considered persona non-grata by the Indian government.

There will always be two sides to a coin, and each person, including this author, has his own biases and prejudices. But to be able to visit such a sensitive border in a time of peace, even be it a temporary peace, is a rare opportunity. I must thank the good fortune bestowed on me by Guru Rinpoche.

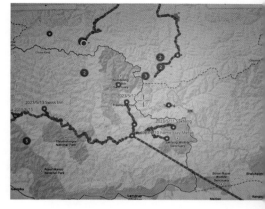

Route of April trip in East Bhutan and current approach to border at 2 & 3 /
四月不丹東部之行的路線，以及目前前往 2 號與 3 號邊境點的路線圖

再訪一觸即發的西藏邊界

勒布溝是克傑朗河上的一處峽谷，那河從西藏南部的錯那縣蜿蜒至印度佔領管轄範圍內的達旺區。峽谷附近不遠處，就是那些一直處於邊界爭議中的中國小村落，北接眾所周知的麥克馬洪線。這些都是門巴族人的村莊，因與邊線南邊相同民族的人們共享著一樣的歷史、文化與宗教遺產而顯得格外重要。而我所在的勒村，正是離邊境線最近的那一個。

十七世紀初，實力強大的第五世達賴喇嘛設立了達旺地區作為拉薩的藩屬國之一，以便收取關稅和朝貢。當時整個地區被稱為門隅，與之相對應的是東邊的另外兩「隅」，察隅和珞隅。這裡的居民主要是門巴族，還有些珞巴族和藏族。正是在這樣錯綜複雜的地域脈絡中，誕生了詩意與浪漫的化身，第六世達賴倉央嘉措。

位於塔希岡省的梅拉克和薩克騰兩地，原本屬於達旺的一部分，曾被視為中國與不丹之間未明確界定且有爭議的領土，但後來英國殖民政府退出後，這片土地被印度慷慨地「給予」了不丹。如今，它看起來已然是不丹的實際領土。然而在二〇二〇年，正當不丹開始準備設立薩克騰野生動物保護區時，中國提出了異議，認為該區的使用權仍有待商榷。

Snow range along road / 沿路的積雪

一個月前，我有幸訪問了邊界另一側的不丹，而現在我在西藏自治區，三國會合之地，看似河清海晏，但只能在心裡默默祈禱這不是暴風雨來臨前的寧靜。最近，甚至有傳言稱，經過二十多輪的談判，中國已傾向接受梅拉克和薩克騰屬於不丹國界，一切就按著現在的國界地圖來定。據說，這是中國回報給不丹放棄另一塊數百平方公里爭議領土的禮物，該領土位於我目前所在的勒村附近的南部。沒辦法，危險又迷人的探險家總會被捲入邊境爭議地區，還能自由穿梭於邊界的兩側。

透過外交交流和談判，中國在過去幾十年間解決了多個與鄰國的領土爭端，通常情況下都是以土地換和平。中國在外交方面可謂是條靈活的變色龍，在與些微小國家的交往中，中國的形象是慷慨解囊，友善以待的「施予者」。然而，面對那些強大的對手時，中國的態度又能做到一百八十度大轉彎，強硬且自信滿滿。就像現今南海與台灣問題正處於白熱化階段，世界上人口最稠密的兩個大國之間的博弈卻遲遲沒有結論，誰也不想先讓一步。但其實想想也知道，中國從過去的經歷中吸取了

Menpa Quzhoung of Le / 勒村的門巴族人
Tea grower Menpa of Le / 種茶的村民

不少經驗。那些微小的邊境摩擦，如果雙方做不到冷靜地去商榷，很可能會將問題擴大化到兩邊都撈不到好處的地步。一九八七年我最後一次訪問錯那時，正趕上那樣一個劍拔弩張的時刻，當時中印邊界的兩側都部署了嚴密的軍隊，感覺戰爭要一觸即發。

我們從海拔五千多米的雲端仙境躍下，走進了喜馬拉雅山南坡海拔不逾三千米的森林懷抱。這裡叫瑪瑪鄉與勒村，又稱勒鄉村。從這裡到薩克騰直線距離不足五十公里，到塔希央奇則是四十公里，到達旺更近，只要三十公里。帶著我的邊境通行證，我的隊伍就能探訪最接近邊界線的各個區域。我想去拜一座小廟，傳說那裡是寧瑪派創始人蓮花生大師曾經坐禪待過的地方，他還在那裡留下了一頂舊帽。相傳，蓮花生大師從印度來到西藏時，降伏了當地的邪惡女巫，現在那個女巫的化石骨頭還在那邊的岩石中清晰可見。圍繞著這個遺址，還有許多關於蓮花生大師的其他遺跡，廟外都有圖文並茂的指示牌用於解說。

攀登至小巧的錫如努迦神殿大約只需要半小時。我混在幾組從拉薩來的藏族朝聖者之間，與他們不約而同地躲避著野猴群。因為有些遊客有餵食或戲弄牠們的壞習慣，這些猴子有時便會明目張膽地騷擾來訪者。這裡的看守者只有一位名叫阿旺歐色的老喇嘛，他不喜歡被拍照，也不太願意與遊客有過多的交流。我的研究助理措姆是藏族人，她設法說服了老僧打開神龕的門鎖讓我們

快速瞥見了一下內在。廟旁有一道美麗的瀑布傾瀉而下，太陽的光芒在水花飛濺中照射出斑斕的彩虹。

途中我們遇到了四十三歲的曲布瓊，今天是她負責清掃通向寺廟及其周圍的石徑。這樣的志願服務是由勒村的村民們輪流進行的。曲布瓊和四十七歲的丈夫多博吉育有三個孩子，大兒子已從大學畢業，在鄰村當祕書，次子仍在讀大學三年級，收養的女兒也是大學畢業生，所以我想他倆肯定既驕傲又滿足。在如今的中國，從前貧困的邊遠地區有這樣的向好變化越來越常見。比如這裡的許多門巴族人都參與了社區茶葉種植與加工合作社。他們村產的優質茶葉供不應求，在整個西藏地區都很流行。

現在的勒村有三十二戶人家，成年人超過七十位。自二〇一七年起，政府執行新政策，旨在提升西藏國界線附近六百二十八個小村莊的基本繁榮水平。勒村正是受惠於此政策的村落之一。

該政策主打提供潔淨飲水、電力、道路通達、科學與人文教育、醫療衛生條件的改善。在新建的房屋中，政府出資百分之七十，當地居民只需負擔百分之三十。他們在原村址上重建，打造別墅式的家庭住宅。一些較小且偏遠的家庭也在政府的安排下遷移到新村莊。大家都希望神聖的邊境寺廟能帶來朝聖者和遊客，從而也給村民帶來一定的收入。

在過去，邊境的門巴族人之間偶爾會有貿易往來，達旺地區也有少量來到中國的朝聖者。然而自從新冠疫情爆發，這些活動都已經停止且尚未恢復。在我看來，將一些有地緣政治爭議的地區開發為特殊的緩衝區，兩國在多個方面協同合作管理，或許可以成為未來鄰國之間緩和關係的對策。畢竟，鄰居永遠不會消失，他們最終還是要學會與彼此和平相處，不論歷史、文化、宗教或政治上有多少

相似，又有多少不同。

在訪問邊境地區的空隙，我們在克節朗河邊的峽谷旁露營了兩晚，這裡也是一九六二年張國華將軍發動中印之戰時的野戰司令部所在地。在中國，這場戰役被稱為克節朗之役，自十月十五日起，歷九日至十月二十四日結束。

那次戰役人民解放軍斬釘截鐵地向達旺平原推進，消滅了印方的前鋒軍，然後單方面宣布停火，並撤回到以前的控制線。顯然，他們在戰場上已經明確表達了立場。自那以後，兩國關係一直較為冷淡，再也未曾回到二十世紀五〇年代的蜜月期。今天，河的對岸有一座小型博物館，裡面重現了那場戰役的營地模型。

國家與國家之間的互相指控永遠不會結束，就像不同的人站在不同的立場，看待問題的角度又怎會一樣。我認為澳洲記者奈維・麥斯威爾在其開創性的著作《印度對華戰爭》中其實已經算相對清醒地保持了中立立場，但仍有大批「公知」覺得這本書是「修正主義」的典型。這本書的創作背景正是中印衝突爆發時，當時麥斯威爾受僱於《倫敦時報》，前往印度當駐外戰地記者。當他在獲得印度軍方的機密文件——亨德森－布魯克斯報告後，重新審視了自己的觀念和視角，寫下了這本讓他幾十年來一直受印度政府白眼的著作。

不過話說回來，硬幣永遠有兩面，每個人，包括我在內，都有其偏見與成見，這是人性，無法避免。現在我只想著，在和平時期，即使或許只是暫時性的和平，能夠造訪如此敏感的邊境地帶，實屬難得。在此，我必須鄭重感謝蓮花生大師賜予我的好運！

Gorge of the Namka Chu / 克節朗河邊的峽谷

依揚想亮 出版書目

國家圖書館出版品預行編目 (CIP) 資料

齊物逍遙 . 2024. I = Enlightened sojourn/ 黃效文著 . -- 初版 .
-- 新北市 : 依揚想亮人文事業有限公司 , 2024.09
面 ; 公分
中英對照
ISBN 978-626-96174-6-3(精裝)
1.CST: 遊記 2.CST: 世界地理
719   113012830

齊
物
逍
遙 2024 I

作者 · 黃效文 | 攝影 · 黃效文 | 發行人 · 劉鋆 | 美術編輯 · Rene、鍾京燕 | 責任編輯 · 廖又蓉 | 翻譯 ·
童貴珊、呂怡達 | 法律顧問 · 達文西個資暨高科技法律事務所 | 出版社 · 依揚想亮人文事業有限公司 |
經銷商 · 聯合發行股份有限公司 | 地址 · 新北市新店區寶橋路 235 巷 6 弄 6 號 2 樓 | 電話 · 02 2917
8022 | 印刷 · 禹利電子分色有限公司 | 初版一刷 · 2024 年 9 月 (精裝) | 定價 1500 元 | ISBN · 978-626-
96174-6-3 | 版權所有　翻印必究 | Print in Taiwan